to

"LITTLE THÉRÈSE"

and

MOTHER AGNES OF JESUS

a little tribute of
reverent and loving gratitude
from the Carmel of Kilmacud

June 9, 1914

St. Thérèse of the Child Jesus
The Little Flower
1873–1897

THOUGHTS OF ST. THÉRÈSE OF THE CHILD JESUS

The Little Flower of Jesus
Carmelite of the Monastery of Lisieux
1873-1897

Translated from the
French *Pensées* by an Irish Carmelite

TAN Books
Gastonia, North Carolina

Nihil Obstat
Remigius Lafort, S.T.D.
Censor

Imprimatur
✠ John Cardinal Farley
Archbishop of New York
October 22, 1915

This edition of *The Thoughts of St. Thérèse of the Child Jesus* was retypeset from the edition published by P. J. Kenedy & Sons, New York, 1915, and republished in 2026 by TAN Books.

Cover design by Caroline Green

Cover image: Portrait of Saint-Thérèse by F. Roytelet. Baron Gerard's gift to Carmelites at Lisieux (1917). Photo by G. Dagli Orti /© NPL - DeA Picture Library / Bridgeman Images.

ISBN: 978-1-5051-3906-8
ePUB ISBN: 978-1-5051-3907-5

Published in the United States by
TAN Books
PO Box 269
Gastonia, NC 28053

www.TANBooks.com

Printed in the United States of America

Contents

About St. Thérèse

SAINT Thérèse of the Child Jesus, known as "The Little Flower," was born January 2, 1873 and baptized Marie-Francoise Thérèse Martin. She grew up surrounded by the love of her parents and her four older sisters, who taught her very early to love God. Thérèse's mind awakened at an early age; she was later to say, "From the age of three I have never refused the good God anything."

When Thérèse was four and a half years old, her beloved mother died, beginning a most painful time in Thérèse's life. She became shy and overly sensitive and would cry at the least provocation, despite her valiant efforts at self-mastery. Then at the age of ten she experienced a mysterious illness; this was cured through the miraculous smile of a statue of the Blessed Mother.

Thérèse's cure of over-sensitiveness came on Christmas night when she was almost 14; in an instant she regained the strength of soul for which she had vainly striven during nearly ten years. Thérèse considered this experience to have been her "conversion"; from that time forward she made great strides in the spiritual life, unfettered by preoccupations with self. Thérèse saw clearly that the entire spiritual life can be summed up in love.

Entering the Carmelite convent in Lisieux at the age of 15, she received the name Sister Thérèse of the Child Jesus; soon she was allowed to add to it "and the Holy Face." Thérèse had great desires for holiness. She admired the great St. Joan of Arc, yet she knew her own path to holiness was to be that of embracing her own littleness and making continual efforts to love God in everything she did, even in very little matters. She would place all her confidence in God, trusting Him to give the victory she was unable to achieve by herself. Thérèse summed up this way of holiness as her "Little Way of Spiritual Childhood."

Recognizing Thérèse's spiritual wisdom, her superiors placed her in charge of the novices when she was only 20. She was also filled with far-reaching desires to be a missionary, an apostle, and a martyr, but she knew that God meant these desires to be fulfilled in a hidden, spiritual manner, through prayer, acts of obedience and daily sacrifice performed faithfully with great love for Him. She offered herself to God as a victim of holocaust to Merciful Love, in order that her life might be "one act of perfect love."

When Thérèse was about 22, her health began to fail from tuberculosis. Though her physical suffering became intense, she suffered spiritually even more, undergoing a darkness of soul in which God and eternity seemed like a hoax. The thought of Heaven, which had always attracted her heart and given her joy and hope, faded into nothingness. She clung to God in sheer faith. Yet during this time, as throughout her life, Thérèse's hallmark was a constant smile. Pointing to a bottle of brightly colored medicine, she once remarked that her life was similar: appearing sweet and delicious on the outside, but in reality very bitter. Yet she also said that she was always happy; she knew that God loved her and that He would make fruitful her own efforts to love Him unto folly.

Thérèse died on September 30, 1897 at the age of 24, having promised to send down from Heaven a "shower of roses" after her death. Almost immediately after she died, many people began learning about her, praying to her and receiving favors from her—then clamoring to the Church authorities for her canonization. Thérèse's account of her life, entitled Story of a Soul, which had been written under obedience, soon was translated into many languages and became known all over the world.

St. Thérèse was canonized by Pope Pius XI in 1925. And in 1927, although she had never left her convent, St. Thérèse was proclaimed co-patron of the missions along with the great St. Francis Xavier, the Apostle of the Indies, who had converted hundreds of thousands.

The Church has affirmed the value of St. Thérèse's "Little Way," proclaiming it to be an excellent way of holiness for all. Pope St. Pius X called St. Thérèse "the greatest saint of modern times" and in 1997, the centenary of her death, Pope St. John Paul II declared her a Doctor of the Church (the youngest to receive this honor) for her spiritual doctrine.

—TAN Books and Publishers, Inc.

Thoughts of Saint Thérèse of the Child Jesus

I

Love of God

JESUS! . . . I would so love Him! Love Him as never yet He has been loved. . .

Letter IV to Mother Agnes of Jesus (Her sister Pauline.)

THE science of love! Sweet is the echo of that word to the ear of my soul. I desire no other science. *Having given all my substance for it*, like the spouse in the Canticles, *I think that I have given nothing.*[1]

Story of a Soul, *Ch. VIII*

WITHOUT love, deeds, even the most brilliant, count as nothing.

Story of a Soul, *Ch. VIII*

[1] Cant. viii, 7.

ONE evening, at a loss for words to tell Jesus how I loved Him and how much I wished that He might be everywhere served and glorified, I reflected with pain that not one act of love would ever mount upwards from out of the depths of hell. Then I cried out that willingly would I consent to see myself plunged into that place of torment and blasphemy, in order that He might be loved there eternally. That could not really glorify Him since He desires only our happiness, but love makes one want to say a thousand foolish things. If I spoke thus, it was not that I did not long for heaven; but then, my heaven was none other than *Love*, and in my fervor I felt that nothing could separate me from the Divine object of my love. . .

Story of a Soul, *Ch. V*

SEEING the eternal recompense so disproportionate to the trifling sacrifices of this life, I longed to love Jesus, to love Him ardently, to give Him a thousand proofs of tenderness while yet I could do so. . .

Story of a Soul, *Ch. V*

THE love of God reveals itself in the very simplest soul who resists His grace in nothing, as well as in the most sublime. Indeed, the characteristic of love being to humble itself, if all souls resembled those of the holy Doctors who have enlightened the Church, the good God would not seem to descend low enough in coming to them. But He has created the infant who knows nothing and can only wail; He has created the poor savage who has but the natural law for guidance, and it is even unto their hearts that He deigns to stoop.

Story of a Soul, *Ch. I*

IN order that Love may be fully satisfied it must needs stoop to very nothingness and transform that nothing into fire.

Story of a Soul, *Ch. XI*

IN times of aridity when I am incapable of praying, of practicing virtue, I seek little opportunities, mere trifles, to give pleasure to Jesus; for instance a smile, a pleasant word when inclined to be silent and to show weariness. If I find no opportunities, I at least tell Him again and again that I love Him; that is not difficult and it keeps alive the fire in my heart. Even though this fire of love might seem to me extinct I would still throw little straws upon the embers and I am certain it would rekindle.

Letter XVI to her Sister Celine

ON *the day of my conversion* Charity entered into my heart and with it a yearning to forget self always; thenceforward I was happy.

Story of a Soul, *Ch. V*

I DO not will that creatures should possess a single atom of my love; I wish to give all to Jesus, since He makes me understand that He alone is perfect happiness. All shall be for Him, all! And even when I have nothing to offer Him I will give Him that nothing.

Letter II to Mother Agnes of Jesus

OUR Lord is more tender than a mother, and well do I know more than one maternal heart! I know a mother is ever ready to forgive the little involuntary failings of her child.

Story of a Soul, *Ch. VIII*

I KNOW of one means only by which to attain to perfection: LOVE. Let us love, since our heart is made for nothing else. Sometimes I seek another word to express Love, but in this land of exile *the word which begins and ends*[2] is quite incapable of rendering the vibrations of the soul; we must then adhere to this simple and only word: TO LOVE.

But on whom shall our poor heart lavish its love? Who shall be found that is great enough to be the recipient of its treasures? Will a human being know how to comprehend them, and above all will he be able to repay? There exists but one Being capable of comprehending love; it is Jesus; He alone can give us back infinitely more than we shall ever give to Him.

Letter to her Cousin Marie Guerin

---

2 St. Augustine.

THERE is one ONLY THING to do here below: to love Jesus, to win souls for Him so that He may be loved. Let us seize with jealous care every least opportunity of self-sacrifice. Let us refuse Him nothing—He does so want our love!

Letter VI to her Sister Celine

WHEN we really love, we rejoice in the happiness of the loved one and make every sacrifice to procure it for him.

Counsels and Reminiscences

TRUE love is nourished by sacrifice, and the more the soul denies itself natural satisfactions, the stronger and the more disinterested becomes its tenderness.

Counsels and Reminiscences

THE good God does not need years to accomplish His work of love in a soul; one ray from His Heart can, in an instant, make His flower bloom for eternity. . .

Letter VI to her Sister Celine

LOVE can supply for length of years. Jesus, because He is Eternal, regards not the time but only the love.

Letter V to Mother Agnes of Jesus

I DESIRE no sensible consolation in loving; provided Jesus feel my love that is enough for me. Oh! to love Him and to make Him loved . . . how sweet it is. . .

Letter V to Mother Agnes of Jesus

O JESUS, I ask of Thee only Peace! . . . Peace, and above all LOVE—love without bound or limit. Jesus, let me for Thy sake die a martyr; give me martyrdom of soul or body. Ah! rather give me both the one and the other!

Story of a Soul, *Ch. VIII*

I HAVE no longer any desire unless it be to love Jesus even to folly! Yes, LOVE it is that draws me. I can say these words of the canticle of our Father, St. John of the Cross:

In the inmost cellar
Of my Beloved have I drunk; and when I went forth
Over all the plain
I knew nothing,
And lost the flock I followed before.
My soul is occupied
And all my substance in His service;
Now I guard no flock,
Nor have I any other employment:
My sole occupation is love.
(*Spiritual Canticle,* Trans. D. Lewis.)

Story of a Soul, *Ch. VIII*

OH! if souls weak and imperfect as mine, felt what I feel, not one would despair of reaching the summit of the mountain of Love, since Jesus does not demand from us great deeds, but only self-surrender and gratitude.

I have no need, saith He, *of the goats of thy flocks . . . If I were hungry I would not tell thee . . . Offer unto God the sacrifice of praise and thanksgiving.*[3]

See then, all that Jesus asks of us! He has not need of our works but only of our *love.* This very God who declares that He needs not to tell us if He were hungry, did not hesitate to *beg* of the Samaritan woman a little water . . . He thirsted!!! But in saying: *"Give me to drink,"*[4] it was the love of His poor creature that the Creator of the universe besought. He thirsted for Love!

And now, more than ever is Jesus athirst. He meets with none but the ungrateful and the indifferent among the disciples of the world; and amongst *His own* disciples He finds, alas! very few hearts that surrender themselves without any reserve to the tenderness of His infinite Love.

Story of a Soul, *Ch. XI*

Since ever I have known Love's mighty power
Thus hath it wrought its work within my soul—
Whate'er it findeth there, or good or ill,
It turneth all to gain; its living flame
Transforms my soul into its very self.[5]

---

3 *Cf.* Ps., xlix, 9, 12, 14.

4 John, iv, 7.

5 St. John of the Cross.

HOW sweet is the way of Love! True, one may fall, one may not be always faithful, but Love, knowing how to draw profit from all, very quickly consumes whatsoever may displease Jesus, leaving naught but humble and profound peace in the innermost soul.

Story of a Soul, *Ch. VIII*

THINKING one day of those who offer themselves as victims to the Justice of God in order to turn aside the punishment reserved for sinners by taking it upon themselves, I felt this offering to be noble and generous, but I was far from feeling moved to make it.

"O my Divine Master," I cried in the depths of my heart, "shall Thy Justice alone receive victims of holocaust? Has not Thy Merciful Love also need of them? On all sides it is ignored, rejected . . . the hearts on which Thou wouldst lavish it turn to creatures, seeking happiness in miserable and fleeting affections instead of casting themselves into Thine arms, into the ineffable furnace of Thine Infinite Love.

"O my God, must Thy Love—disdained—remain within Thy Heart? Methinks that if Thou shouldst find souls offering themselves as victims of holocaust to Thy

Love, Thou wouldst consume them rapidly; that Thou wouldst be glad not to restrict the flames of infinite tenderness pent up within Thee.

"If Thy Justice—the Justice which Thou dost exercise on earth—be pleased to find voluntary victims on which to discharge its weight, how much the more must Thy Merciful Love also desire its victims, since *Thy Mercy reacheth even to heaven.*[6]

"O Jesus, that happily I may be that holocaust consume Thy little victim in the fire of Divine Love."

Story of a Soul, *Ch. VIII*

AH! since that day love penetrates me and surrounds me; this *Merciful Love* each moment renews and purifies me, leaving in my heart no trace of sin. No, I cannot fear Purgatory; I know that I do not merit even to enter with the Holy Souls into that place of expiation, but I know too that the fire of Love is more sanctifying than the fire of Purgatory, I know that Jesus cannot will needless suffering for us, and that He would not inspire me with the desires I feel if He were unwilling to fulfil them.

Story of a Soul, *Ch. VIII*

---

6 *Cf.* Ps., xxxv, 6.

TO offer oneself as a Victim to Divine Love is not to offer oneself to sweetness—to consolation; but to every anguish, every bitterness, for Love lives only by sacrifice; and the more a soul wills to be surrendered to Love, the more must she be surrendered to suffering.

Story of a Soul, *Ch. XII*

IN order to love Jesus, to be His victim of love, the more weak and miserable we are, the more fitting are we for the operations of this consuming and transforming Love . . . The sole desire to be victim suffices; but we must consent to remain always poor and without strength, and there lies the difficulty, for *where shall be found the truly poor in spirit? He must be sought afar off,*[7] saith the author of the *Imitation*. . . He did not say that we must seek him amongst great souls, but afar off, that is to say in lowliness, in nothingness . . . Oh! let us keep *afar off* from all that glitters, let us love our littleness, and be satisfied to feel nothing, then shall we be truly poor in spirit, and Jesus will come to seek us how far soever we may be; He will transform us into flames of Love! . . .

Letter to Sister Marie of the Sacred Heart (her Sister Marie.)

---

7 *Cf.* The Imitation of Christ, II, xi, 4.

TO be truly a Victim of Love requires absolute self-surrender. *The soul is consumed by Love only in so far as she surrenders herself to Love.*

Counsels and Reminiscences

IT appears to me that for Victims of Love there will be no judgment, but rather, that the good God will hasten to recompense with eternal delights His own Love, which He will see burning in their hearts.

Counsels and Reminiscences

AT any cost I will cull the palm of Saint Agnes; if not by shedding my blood then it must be by Love. . .

Letter IV to Mother Agnes of Jesus

O MY God, Thou knowest I have never desired but to love Thee alone. I seek no other glory. Thy Love has gone before me from my childhood, it has grown with my growth, and now it is an abyss the depths of which I cannot fathom.

Story of a Soul, *Ch. XI*

LOVE attracts love, mine rushes forth unto Thee, it would fain fill up the abyss which attracts it; but alas! it is not even as one drop of dew lost in the Ocean. To love Thee as Thou lovest me I must borrow Thy very love—then only, can I find rest.

Story of a Soul, *Ch. XI*

JUST as a torrent sweeps along with it unto the depths of the sea whatsoever it encounters on its course, even so, my Jesus, does the soul which plunges into the boundless ocean of Thy Love draw after her all her treasures. Lord, Thou knowest that for me these treasures are the souls it has pleased Thee to unite to mine.

Story of a Soul, *Ch. XI*

CHARITY gave me the key to my vocation. I understood that the Church being a body composed of different members, the most essential, the most noble of all the organs would not be wanting to her; I understood that the Church has *a heart* and that this heart is burning with love; that it is love alone which makes the members work, that if love were to die away apostles would no longer preach the Gospel, martyrs would refuse to shed their blood. I understood that love comprises all vocations, that love is everything, that it embraces all times and all places because it is eternal!

Story of a Soul, *Ch. XI*

O MY Well-Beloved! I understand to what combats Thou hast destined me; it is not on the battle field that I shall fight . . . I am prisoner of Thy Love; freely have I riveted the chain which unites me to Thee and separates me forever from the world. My sword is LOVE; with it *I shall chase the stranger from the kingdom, I shall make Thee to be proclaimed King* in the souls of men.

Story of a Soul, *Appendix*

LOVE! . . . that is what I ask . . . I know but one thing now—*to love Thee*, O Jesus! Glorious deeds are not for me, I cannot preach the Gospel, shed my blood . . . what does it matter? My brothers toil instead of me, and I, *the little child*, I keep quite close to the royal throne, *I love* for those who fight.

Story of a Soul, *Ch. XI*

HOW shall I show my love since love is proved by deeds? Well,—*the little child will strew flowers* . . . she will embalm the Divine Throne with their fragrance, will sing with silvery voice the canticle of love.

Yes, my Beloved, it is thus that my life's brief day shall be spent before Thee. No other means have I of proving my love than to strew flowers; that is, to let no little sacrifice escape me, not a look, not a word, to avail of the very least actions and do them for Love. I wish to suffer for Love's sake and for Love's sake even to rejoice; thus shall I strew flowers. Not one shall I find without shedding its petals for Thee . . . and then I will sing, I will always sing, even if I must gather my roses in the very midst of thorns—and the longer and sharper the thorns the sweeter shall be my song.

Story of a Soul, *Ch. XI*

SAINT Thérèse of the Child Jesus often spoke of a well-known toy with which in childhood's days she had amused herself: a kaleidoscope; in form somewhat like a small telescope; on looking through, one sees an endless succession of pretty and many-colored designs, varying at each turn of the kaleidoscope.

"This toy," she said, "aroused my admiration and I used to wonder what could produce so pleasing a phenomenon; when one day, after serious examination, I saw there were simply a few tiny scraps of paper and of wool cut no matter how, and thrown here and there. I pursued my investigation and discovered three mirrors inside the tube: I had there the key to the problem.

"This was for me the image of a great mystery. As long as our actions, even the least of them, remain within the focus of Love, the Blessed Trinity, which is figured by the three mirrors, reflects them, and endows them with a wondrous beauty. Jesus, looking at us through the little lens, that is to say, as it were through Himself, finds all our actions pleasing to Him. But if we leave the ineffable centre of Love, what will He see? Mere straws . . . actions sullied and nothing worth."

Counsels and Reminiscences

THIS little prayer which includes all my desires I ask you to say for me each day:

"Merciful Father, in the name of Thy sweet Jesus, of the Blessed Virgin and of the Saints, I pray Thee that my sister be fired with Thy spirit of love, and that Thou wilt grant her the grace to make Thee greatly loved."

If God should take me soon to Himself, I ask you to continue each day this same prayer, for in Heaven my desire will be the same as upon earth; to love Jesus and to make Him loved.

Letter III to her Missionary "Brothers"

SHE was looking at the sky one day when some one remarked to her:

"Very soon you will dwell beyond the blue sky; with what love you contemplate it!"

She merely smiled, but afterwards said to the Mother Prioress:

"Mother, our Sisters little know what I suffer! Looking at the blue sky I was thinking only of the beauty of the material heavens; *the other is more and more closed to me* . . . I was at first distressed by that remark, then an interior voice answered: 'Yes, through love thou didst look at the heavens. Since thy soul is wholly consecrated to Love, all thy actions, even the most indifferent, bear the impress of this divine seal.' I was instantly consoled."

Story of a Soul, *Ch. XII*

UNTIL two days before her death she wished to be alone at night, however, notwithstanding her entreaties, the Infirmarian used to rise several times to visit her. On one occasion she found our little invalid with hands clasped and eyes raised to Heaven.

"But what are you doing?" she asked; "you should try to sleep."

"I cannot, dear Sister, I suffer too much! then I pray. . ."

"And what do you say to Jesus?"

"I say nothing, *I love Him!*"

Story of a Soul, *Ch. XII*

A SISTER was speaking to her of the happiness of Heaven: Thérèse interrupted, saying:

"It is not that which attracts me. . ."

"What is it then?"

"Oh! it is LOVE! To love, to be beloved, and *to come back to earth to make* LOVE *loved.*"

Story of a Soul, *Ch. XII*

LOVE alone have I ever given to the good God, with love He will repay me.

Story of a Soul, *Ch. XII*

ALL that I have written regarding my desire of suffering is most true; oh! I do not repent of having surrendered myself to Love.

Story of a Soul, *Ch. XII*

JESUS! Jesus! if it be so sweet to desire Thy Love, what will it be to possess and to enjoy it forever!

Story of a Soul, *Ch. XI*

O JESUS! could I but tell all *little souls* of Thine ineffable condescension! . . . I feel that if it were possible to find one more weak than mine Thou wouldst take delight in showering upon her greater favors still, provided that she abandoned herself with entire confidence to Thine Infinite Mercy.

But why these desires, O my Beloved, to impart the secrets of Thy Love? Is it not Thyself alone Who hast made them known to me and canst Thou not reveal them to others? Yes, I know it and I implore Thee to *do* so: *I beseech Thee to let Thy divine gaze rest upon an immense number of little souls, I beseech Thee to choose in this world a Legion of little victims worthy of Thy Love!*

Story of a Soul, *Ch. XI*

HER last words—looking at her crucifix: "OH! . . . I LOVE HIM! . . . MY GOD, I . . . LOVE . . . THEE!!!"

Story of a Soul, *Ch. XII*

O MY God, Most Blessed Trinity, I desire to love Thee and to make Thee loved, to labour for the glory of Holy Church by saving souls still on earth and by delivering those who suffer in purgatory. I desire to accomplish Thy Will perfectly, and to attain to the degree of glory which Thou hast prepared for me in Thy Kingdom, in one word, I desire to be a saint, but I know that I am powerless, and I implore Thee, O my God, to be Thyself my sanctity.

Since Thou hast so loved me as to give me Thine only Son to be my Saviour and my Spouse, the infinite treasures of His merits are mine, to Thee I offer them with joy, beseeching Thee to see me only as in the Face of Jesus and in His Heart burning with Love.

Again, I offer Thee all the merits of the Saints—in Heaven and on earth—their acts of love and those of the holy Angels; and finally I offer Thee, O Blessed Trinity, the love and the merits of the Holy Virgin, my most dear Mother; it is to her I entrust my oblation, begging her to present it to Thee.

Her Divine Son, my well-beloved Spouse, during His life on earth, told us: *"If you ask the Father anything in My Name He will give it to you."*[8] I am then certain that Thou wilt hearken to my desires . . . My God, I know it, the more Thou willest to give the more dost

---

[8] John, xvi, 23.

Thou make us desire. Immense are the desires that I feel within my heart, and it is with confidence that I call upon Thee to come and take possession of my soul. I cannot receive Thee in Holy Communion as often as I would; but, Lord, art Thou not Almighty? . . . Remain in me as in the Tabernacle—never leave Thy little Victim.

I long to console Thee for the ingratitude of the wicked and I pray Thee take from me the liberty to displease Thee! If through frailty I fall sometimes, may Thy Divine glance purify my soul immediately, consuming every imperfection—like to fire which transforms all things into itself.

I thank Thee, O my God, for all the graces Thou hast bestowed on me, and particularly for making me pass through the crucible of suffering. It is with joy I shall behold Thee on the Last Day bearing Thy scepter—the Cross; since Thou hast deigned to give me for my portion this most precious Cross, I have hope of resembling Thee in Heaven and seeing the sacred stigmata of Thy Passion shine in my glorified body.

After exile on earth I hope to enjoy the possession of Thee in our eternal Fatherland, but I have no wish to amass merits for Heaven, I will work for Thy Love alone, my sole aim being to give Thee pleasure, to console Thy Sacred Heart, and to save souls who will love Thee forever.

At the close of life's evening I shall appear before Thee with empty hands, for I ask not, Lord, that Thou wouldst count my works . . . All our justice is tarnished in Thy sight. It is therefore my desire to be clothed with Thine own Justice and to receive from Thy Love the eternal possession of Thyself. I crave no other Throne nor other Crown but Thee, O my Beloved! . . .

In Thy sight time is nothing, *one day is as a thousand years.*[9] Thou canst in an instant prepare me to appear before Thee. That I may live in one Act of perfect Love, I OFFER MYSELF AS A VICTIM OF HOLOCAUST TO THY MERCIFUL LOVE, imploring Thee to consume me without ceasing, and to let the tide of infinite tenderness pent up in Thee, overflow into my soul, that so I may become a very martyr of Thy Love, O my God!

May this martyrdom, having first prepared me to appear before Thee, break life's thread at last, and may my soul take its flight, *unretarded*, into the eternal embrace of Thy Merciful Love.

---

9 *Cf.* Ps., lxxxix, 4.

I desire, O Well-Beloved, at every heart-beat to renew this Oblation an infinite number of times, *till the shadows retire*[10] and I can tell Thee my love eternally face to face!

(Signed)

MARIE-FRANÇOISE-THÉRÈSE DE L'ENFANT JÉSUS ET DE LA SAINTE FACE

Rel. Carm. ind.

Feast of The Most Holy Trinity.
The 9th of June in the year of grace, 1895.

[10] Cant., iv, 6.

II

Love of Our Neighbor

THERE are moments when we are so wretched within, that we must needs hurry away from ourselves. The good God does not oblige us to remain at such times in our own company; indeed He often permits that it should be displeasing to us just that we may leave it. And I see no other means of going out of ourselves than by going to visit Jesus and Mary, that is, hastening to deeds of charity.

Counsels and Reminiscences

I APPLIED myself above all to practise quite hidden little acts of virtue; thus I liked to fold the mantles forgotten by the Sisters, and sought a thousand opportunities of rendering them service.

Story of a Soul, *Ch. VII*

HAD I been rich I never could have borne to see a poor person hungry without giving him to eat. It is the same in my spiritual life: knowing there are souls on the point of falling into Hell, I give them my treasures according as I earn anything, and I have never yet found a moment to say: "Now I am going to work for myself."

Counsels and Reminiscences

I FEEL that when I am charitable it is Jesus alone who acts in me; the more I am united to Him the more do I love all my Sisters. If, when I desire to increase this love in my heart, the demon tries to set before my eyes the faults of one or other of the Sisters, I hasten to call to mind her virtues, her good desires; I say to myself that if I have seen her fall once, she may well have gained many victories which she conceals through humility; and that even what appears to me a fault may in truth be an act of virtue by reason of the intention.

Story of a Soul, *Ch. IX*

TRUE Charity consists in bearing with all the defects of our neighbor, in not being surprised at his failings, and in being edified by his least virtues; Charity must not remain shut up in the depths of the heart, for *no man lighteth a candle and putteth it under a bushel, but upon a candlestick, that it may shine to all that are in the house.*[11] It seems to me that this candle represents the Charity which ought to enlighten and make joyful, not only those who are dearest to me, but *all who are in the house.*

Story of a Soul, *Ch. IX*

THERE is no artist who does not like his work praised, and the Divine Artist of souls is pleased when we do not stop at the exterior, but penetrating even to the inmost sanctuary which He has chosen for His dwelling, we admire its beauty.

Story of a Soul, *Ch. IX*

---

11 *Cf.* Matt., v, 15.

I OUGHT to seek the company of those Sisters who according to nature please me least. I ought to fulfil in their regard the office of the Good Samaritan. A word, a kindly smile, will often suffice to gladden a wounded and sorrowful heart.

Story of a Soul, *Ch. X*

OH! what peace inundates the soul when she rises above natural sentiment. No joy can compare with that known to one who is truly poor in spirit. If he ask with detachment for some necessary thing, and it is not only refused him, but an attempt made besides to deprive him of what he already has, he follows the counsel of our Lord: *"And if a man will contend with thee in judgment and take away thy coat, let go thy cloak also unto him."*[12]

To yield up our cloak means, I think, to renounce our last rights, to consider oneself as the servant, the slave of others. When we have abandoned our mantle it is easier to walk, to run; therefore Jesus adds: *"And whosoever will force thee one mile, go with him other two."*[13]

---

[12] Matt., v, 40.

[13] Matt., v, 41.

It is not enough that I should give to whosoever may ask of me, I must forestall their desires, and show that I feel much gratified, much honored in rendering service; and if they take a thing that I use, I must seem as though glad to be relieved of it.

Story of a Soul, *Ch. IX*

IF it is hard to give to whoever asks, it is still harder to let what belongs to us be taken, without asking it back, or rather, I ought to say it *seems* hard; for *the yoke of the Lord is sweet and light:*[14] when we accept it we feel its sweetness immediately.

Story of a Soul, *Ch. IX*

WHEN Charity is deeply rooted in the soul it shows itself exteriorly: there is so gracious a way of refusing what we cannot give, that the refusal pleases as much as the gift.

Story of a Soul, *Ch. IX*

---

14 *Cf.* Matt., xi, 30.

TO want to persuade our Sisters that they are in the wrong, even when it is perfectly true, is hardly fair, as we are not responsible for their guidance. We must not be *Justices of the peace*, but only *angels of peace*.

Counsels and Reminiscences

JESUS wills that we give alms to Him as to one poor and needy. He puts Himself as it were at our mercy; He will take nothing but what we give Him from our heart, and the very least trifle is precious in His sight. He stretches forth His Hand, this sweet Saviour, to receive of us a little love, so that in the radiant day of Judgment He may be able to address to us those ineffable words: *"Come, ye blessed of My Father; for I was hungry, and you gave Me to eat; I was thirsty, and you gave Me to drink; I was a stranger, and you took Me in; sick and you visited Me; I was in prison, and you came to Me."*[15]

Letter XV to her Sister Celine

---

[15] Matt., xxv, 34–36.

If I were still to live, the office of Infirmarian is the one which would please me most. I would not ask for it, but if it came direct by obedience I should think myself highly privileged. It seems to me that I would discharge its duties with a tender love, thinking always of our Saviour saying: *"I was sick and you visited me."*[16] The Infirmary bell should be for you as Heavenly music. You ought purposely to pass along beneath the windows of the sick to give them facility in calling you and asking your services. Ought you not to consider yourself like a little slave whom everyone has a right to command? If you could but see the Angels who from the heights of Heaven watch you battling in the arena! They await the end of the combat to cover you with flowers and wreaths. The good God does not disdain these combats, unknown and therefore all the more meritorious. *"The patient man is better than the valiant, and he that ruleth his spirit than he that taketh cities."*[17]

By our little acts of charity practised in the shade we convert souls far away, we help missionaries, we win for them abundant alms; and by that means build actual dwellings spiritual and material for our Eucharistic Lord.

Counsels and Reminiscences

---

[16] Matt., xxv, 36.

[17] Prov., xvi, 32.

A NOVICE remarked to St. Thérèse: "I do not like to see others suffer, especially saintly souls." She replied instantly:

"Oh! I am not like you: to see saints suffer never moves me to pity! I know they have the strength to endure, and they thus give great glory to God: but those who are not holy, who know not how to profit by their sufferings, oh! how I pity them; they do indeed arouse my compassion, and I would do all I could to comfort and help them."

Counsels and Reminiscences

SEEING her extreme weakness the doctor ordered some strengthening remedies; St. Thérèse was distressed at first on account of their high price: then she said to us: "I am no longer grieved about taking these costly remedies, for I have been reading that St. Gertrude rejoiced at the thought that all would be to the advantage of those who do us good, since our Lord has said: *'As long as you did it unto one of these My least brethren you did it unto Me.'*"[18]

---

[18] Matt., xxv, 40.

She added: "I am convinced of the uselessness of medicine for the purpose of curing me, but I have made a compact with the good God, that He is to allow some poor Missionaries to profit by it, who have neither time nor means to take care of themselves."

Story of a Soul, *Ch. XII*

REMEMBERING that *Charity covereth a multitude of sins,*[19] I draw from this fruitful mine opened to us by our Lord in His sacred Gospels. I search the depths of His adorable words and cry out with David: *"I have run in the way of Thy commandments when Thou didst enlarge my heart."*[20] And charity alone can enlarge my heart . . .

O Jesus! since this sweet flame consumes it I run with delight in the way of Thy new Commandment, and therein will I run until the blessed day when with Thy Virgin train I shall follow Thee through Thy boundless Realm singing Thy *New Canticle* which must surely be *the Canticle of LOVE.*

Story of a Soul, *Ch. IX*

---

19 Prov., x, 12.

20 Ps., cxviii, 32.

III
Faith

WHAT helps me most when I picture to myself the interior of the Holy Family is to think of a quite ordinary life.

The Blessed Virgin and St. Joseph knew well that Jesus was God, but wondrous things were nevertheless hidden from them and like us they lived by faith. Have you not noticed what is said in the sacred text: *"And they understood not the word that He spoke unto them,"*[21] and these other words no less mysterious: *"His father and mother were wondering at those things which were spoken concerning Him"*?[22] Does not this imply that they heard of something new to them, for this wondering suggests a certain astonishment?

Counsels and Reminiscences

---

21 Luke, ii, 50.

22 Luke, ii, 33.

DURING her temptations against faith she wrote: "I strive to work by faith though bereft of its consolations. I have made more acts of Faith in this last year than during all the rest of my life.

"On each fresh occasion of combat, when the enemy desires to challenge me, I conduct myself valiantly: knowing that to fight a duel is an unworthy act, I turn my back upon the adversary without ever looking him in the face; then I run to my Jesus and tell Him I am ready to shed every drop of blood in testimony of my belief that there is a Heaven, I tell Him I am glad to be unable to contemplate, while on earth, with the eyes of the soul, the beautiful Heaven that awaits me so He will deign to open it for eternity to poor unbelievers."

Story of a Soul, *Ch. IX*

HE whose Heart ever watcheth, taught me, that while for a soul whose faith equals but a tiny grain of mustard seed, he works miracles, in order that this faith which is so weak may be fortified; yet for His intimate friends, for His Mother, He did not work miracles until He had put their faith to the test. Did He not let Lazarus die though Martha and Mary had sent to tell Him that he was sick? At the marriage at Cana, the Blessed Virgin having asked Him to come to the assistance of the Master of the house, did He not reply that His hour was not yet come? But after the trial, what a recompense! Water changed to wine, Lazarus restored to life. . .

Story of a Soul, *Ch. VI*

A SISTER said to her that beautiful Angels clothed in white robes, and of joyous and resplendent countenance, would bear away her soul to Heaven. She replied: "These imaginations do not help me: I can draw no sustenance except from the Truth. God and the Angels are pure Spirits, no one can see them as they really are, with corporal eyes. That is why I have never desired extraordinary favors. I would rather await the Eternal Vision."

Counsels and Reminiscences

I HAVE asked God to send me a beautiful dream to console me when you are gone," said a novice.

"Ah! that is a thing I should never do—ask for consolation! . . . Since you wish to be like me you well know that I say:

Oh! fear not, Lord, that I shall waken Thee: I await in peace th' eternal shore. . .

"It is so sweet to serve the good God in the dark night of trial; we have this life only in which to live by faith."

Counsels and Reminiscences

IV
Hope

TIME is but a shadow, a dream; already God sees us in glory and takes joy in our eternal beatitude. How this thought helps my soul! I understand then why He lets us suffer . . .

Letter VIII to her Sister Celine

A DAY . . . an hour . . . and we shall have reached the port! My God, what shall we see then? What is that life which will never have an end? . . . Jesus will be the soul of our soul. Unfathomable mystery! *"Eye hath not seen, nor ear heard, neither hath it entered into the heart of man what great things God hath prepared for them that love Him."*[23] And this will all come soon—yes, very soon, if we ardently love Jesus.

Letter VI to her Sister Celine

---

[23] I Cor., ii, 9. *Cf.* Is., lxiv, 4.

LIFE is passing, Eternity draws nigh; soon shall we live the very life of God. After having drunk deep at the fount of bitterness, our thirst will be quenched at the very source of all sweetness.

Yes, *the figure of this world passeth away*,[24] soon shall we see new heavens; a more radiant sun will brighten with its splendors, ethereal seas and infinite horizons . . . We shall no longer be prisoners in a land of exile, all will be at an end and with our Heavenly Spouse we shall sail o'er boundless waters: now our *harps are hung upon the willows that border the rivers of Babylon*,[25] but in the day of our deliverance what harmonies will then be heard! With what joy shall we not make every chord of our instruments to vibrate! Today, *we weep remembering Sion . . . how shall we sing the songs of the Lord in a strange land?*[26]

Letter V to her Sister Celine

---

24 I Cor., vii, 31.

25 *Cf.* Ps., cxxxvi, 2.

26 *Cf.* Ps., cxxxvi, 1, 4.

HOW I thirst for Heaven—that blessed habitation where our love for Jesus will have no limit! But to get there we must suffer . . . we must weep . . . Well, I *wish* to suffer all that shall please my Beloved, I wish to let Him do just as He wills with His *"little ball."*

Letter V to Sr. Marie of the Sacred Heart

OH! What mysteries will be revealed to us later . . . How often have I thought that I perhaps owe all the graces showered upon me to the earnest prayer of a little soul whom I shall know only in Heaven. It is God's will that in this world by means of prayer Heavenly treasures should be imparted by souls one to another, so that when they reach the Fatherland they may love one another with a love born of gratitude, with an affection far, far exceeding the most ideal family affection upon earth.

There, we shall meet with no indifferent looks, because all the Saints will be indebted to each other.

No envious glances will be seen; the happiness of every one of the elect will be the happiness of all. With the Martyrs we shall be like to the Martyrs; with the Doctors we shall be as the Doctors; with the Virgins, as the Virgins; and just as the members of a family are proud of one another, so shall we be of our brethren, without the least jealousy.

Who knows even if the joy we shall experience in beholding the glory of the great Saints, and knowing that by a secret dispensation of Providence we have contributed thereunto, who knows if this joy will not be as intense and sweeter perhaps, than the happiness they will themselves possess.

And do you not think that on their side the great Saints, seeing what they owe to quite little souls, will love them with an incomparable love? Delightful and surprising will be the friendships found there—I am sure of it. The favored companion of an Apostle or a great Doctor of the Church, will perhaps be a young shepherd lad; and a simple little child may be the intimate friend of a Patriarch. Oh! how I long to dwell in that Kingdom of Love . . .

Counsels and Reminiscences

A SISTER showed her a photograph representing Joan of Arc consoled in the prison by her Voices. St. Thérèse said: "I too am consoled by an interior voice. The Saints encourage me from above, they say to me: 'So long as thou art in fetters thou canst not fulfil thy mission; but later, after thy death—*then* will be the time of thy conquests.'"

Counsels and Reminiscences

IN Heaven the good God will do all I wish, because I have never done my own will upon earth.

Counsels and Reminiscences

EVEN now I know it; yes, all my hopes will be fulfilled . . . yes . . . the Lord will work wonders for me which will surpass infinitely my immeasurable desires.

Letter VIII to Mother Agnes of Jesus

V
Humility

IT appears to me that humility is the truth. I know not whether I am humble, but I know that I see the truth in all things.

Counsels and Reminiscences

I HAVE understood what true glory is. He whose *Kingdom is not of this world*[27] showed me that the only enviable royalty consists in loving *to be unknown and esteemed as nothing,*[28] and finding our joy in contempt of self. I wished that like the Face of Jesus, mine might be *as it were hidden and despised.*[29] *That none upon earth might esteem me*. I thirsted to suffer and to be forgotten.

Story of a Soul, *Ch. VII*

---

[27] John, xviii, 36.

[28] *Imit.*, I, ii, 3.

[29] Is., liii, 3.

JESUS made me understand that the true, the only glory is that which will last forever; that to attain to it we need not perform wonderful deeds, but rather, those hidden from the eyes of others and from self, so that *the left hand knoweth not what the right hand doth.*[30]

Story of a Soul, *Ch. IV*

Thérèse is weak, very weak; of this she has new and salutary experience every day. But Jesus takes pleasure in teaching her how to *glory in her infirmities.*[31] It is a great grace this, for herein is found peace and tranquillity. When we see ourselves so miserable, we wish no longer to look at self but only on the Well-Beloved.

Letter II to her Cousin Marie Guerin

I AM a *very little* soul who can offer only *very little* things to the good God; yet, it often happens that these little sacrifices which give such peace to the heart escape me; but that does not discourage me, I bear with

---

[30] Matt., vi, 3.

[31] II Cor., xi, 5.

having a little less peace and I try to be more watchful another time.

Story of a Soul, *Ch. X*

VEILED in the white Host, O my Well-Beloved, how meek and humble of heart dost Thou show Thyself to me! Thou couldst not stoop lower to teach me humility, and I, to respond to Thy Love, desire to put myself in the lowest place and share Thy humiliations, that I may *have part with Thee*[32] in the Kingdom of Heaven.

I beseech Thee, my Jesus, to send me some humiliation every time that I shall attempt to put myself above others.

Story of a Soul, *Appendix*

WHAT pleases the good God in my little soul is to see me love my littleness and my poverty, it is seeing the blind trust that I have in His Mercy.

Letter VI to Sr. Marie of the Sacred Heart

---

32 John, xiii, 8.

TO draw near to Jesus we must be so little . . . Oh! how few souls aspire to be little and unknown. . .

Letter XIV to her Sister Celine

I AM no longer surprised at anything, nor do I grieve at seeing that I am frailty itself; on the contrary I glory in it, and expect to discover new imperfections in myself each day. These lights concerning my nothingness do me more good, I affirm, than lights regarding faith.

Story of a Soul, *Ch. IX*

WHEN we commit a fault we must not think it due to a physical cause, such as illness or the weather, we must attribute this fall to our imperfection, but without ever growing discouraged.

Counsels and Reminiscences

SINCE Jesus has gone back to Heaven I can follow Him only by the path He has traced. Oh how luminous are His footprints—diffusing a divine sweetness . . . I have but to glance at the holy Gospels and immediately I inhale the fragrance of the life of Jesus, and I know which side to take. Not to the first place do I run but to the last. I let the Pharisee go up, and full of confidence I repeat the humble prayer of the publican. Above all I copy the example of Magdalene; her amazing, or rather, her loving audacity, which so touched the Heart of Jesus, charms my own.

Story of a Soul, *Ch. XI*

WITH a simplicity that delights me my little Sisters, the novices, tell me of the interior combats I arouse in them, in what way they find me trying; they are no more embarrassed than if it were question of some one else, knowing that by acting thus, they greatly please me.

Ah! truly it is more than a pleasure, it is a delicious feast which replenishes my soul with joy. How can a thing so disagreeable to nature give such happiness? Had I not experienced it I could not have believed it.

One day when I had an ardent desire for humiliation, it happened that a young postulant so fully satisfied it, that the thought of Semei cursing David came to my mind and I repeated interiorly with the holy King: *Yes, it is indeed the Lord who has commanded him to say all these things to me.*[33]

Thus the good God takes care of me. He cannot always offer me the strength-giving bread of exterior humiliation, but from time to time He permits me to feast upon *the crumbs that fall from the table of the children.*[34] How great is His Mercy!

Story of a Soul, *Ch. X*

ALL creatures might incline towards the little flower, admiring it and overwhelming it with their praise, but never would that add a shadow of vain satisfaction to the true joy of knowing itself to be a mere nothing in the sight of God.

Story of a Soul, *Ch. IX*

BECAUSE I was little and weak, Jesus stooped down to me and tenderly instructed me in the secrets of His Love.

Story of a Soul, *Ch. V*

---

33 Kings, xvi, 10.

34 Mark, vii, 28.

I AM too little to have any vanity, I am also too little to know how to turn beautiful phrases so as to make it appear that I have a great deal of humility. I prefer to acknowledge simply that *He that is mighty hath done great things to me*;[35] and the greatest is His having shown me my littleness, my powerlessness for all good.

Story of a Soul, *Ch. IX*

THE only thing not subject to be envied is the lowest place, it is therefore this lowest place alone which is without vanity and affliction of spirit. Still, *the way of a man is not always in his power*[36] and sometimes we are surprised by a desire for that which glitters. Then, let us take our place humbly amongst the imperfect, deeming ourselves little souls whom the good God must sustain at each moment. As soon as He sees us truly convinced of our nothingness and we say to Him: *My foot hath slipped: Thy mercy, O Lord, hath held me up,*[37] He stretches out His Hand to us; but if we *will* attempt to do something grand, even under pretext

---

35 Luke, i, 49.

36 *Cf.* Jer., x, 23.

37 *Cf.* Ps., xciii, 18.

of zeal, He leaves us alone. It is enough therefore that we humble ourselves, and bear our imperfections with sweetness: there, for us, lies true sanctity.

Counsels and Reminiscences

THE most eloquent discourses would be incapable of inspiring one act of love without the grace that moves the heart.

See a beautiful, rose-tinted peach, of so sweet a savor that no craft of confectioner could produce nectar like it. Is it for the peach itself that God has created this lovely color and delicate velvety surface? Is it for the sake of the peach that He has given it so delicious a flavor? No, it is for us; what alone belongs to it and forms the essence of its existence is its stone; it possesses nothing more.

Thus is Jesus pleased to lavish His gifts on some of His creatures, that through them He may draw to Himself other souls; but in His mercy He humiliates them interiorly, and gently constrains them to recognize their nothingness and His Omnipotence. These sentiments form in them, as it were, a kernel of grace, which Jesus hastens to develop for that blessed day when clothed with a beauty, immortal, imperishable, they shall without danger have place at the Celestial banquet.

Letter XVI to her Sister Celine

THE Apostles, without Jesus, labored long—a whole night—without taking any fish; their toil was pleasing to Him but He wished to show that He alone can give anything. He asked only an act of humility: *"Children, have you any meat?"*[38] and St. Peter confesses his helplessness: *"Lord we have labored all night and have taken nothing."*[39] It is enough! The Heart of Jesus is touched . . . Perhaps if the Apostle had taken a few little fishes the Divine Master would not have worked a miracle; but he had *nothing*, and so through God's power and goodness his nets were soon filled with great fishes.

That is just our Lord's way. He gives as God, but He *will* have humility of heart.

Letter XVII to her Sister Celine

---

38 John, xxi, 5.

39 Luke, v, 5.

TO think ourselves imperfect, and others perfect—that is happiness. That creatures should recognize we are without virtue takes nothing from us, makes us no poorer; it is they who by this lose interior joy; for there is nothing sweeter than to think well of our neighbor.

Counsels and Reminiscences

IT is a great joy to me, not only when others find me imperfect, but above all when I feel that so I am: compliments, on the contrary, cause me nothing but displeasure.

Counsels and Reminiscences

A NOVICE confided to her that she made no progress and felt quite discouraged.

"Till the age of fourteen," said Thérèse, "I practised virtue without feeling its sweetness. I wished for suffering but had no thought of finding my joy therein; that is a grace which has been granted me later. My soul was like a beautiful tree whose blossoms no sooner opened than they fell.

"Offer to the good God the sacrifice of never gathering the fruits of your labors. If He so will that during your whole life you feel a repugnance to suffer and to be humiliated, if He permit that all the flowers of your desires and of your good-will fall to earth without fruit, be not troubled. At the moment of your death He will know well how to bring to perfection, in the twinkling of an eye, beautiful fruits on the tree of your soul.

"We read in the Book of Ecclesiasticus: *'There is an inactive man that wanteth help, is very weak in ability, and full of poverty: yet the eye of God hath looked upon him for good, and hath lifted him up from his low estate, and hath exalted his head: and many have wondered at him and have glorified God.*

'Trust in God, and stay in thy place. For it is easy in the eyes of God, on a sudden to make the poor man rich. The blessing of God maketh haste to reward the just, and in a swift hour His blessing beareth fruit!'"[40]

Counsels and Reminiscences

YOU have always been faithful to divine grace, have you not?"

---

[40] Ecclus., xi, 12, 13, 22, 23, 24.

"Yes, since the age of three I have refused nothing to the good God. Yet not mine the glory. See how the setting sun this evening gilds the topmost branches of the trees; even so does my soul appear to you—all bright and gilded, because it is exposed to Love's rays. If the Divine Sun withheld from me His rays, my soul would immediately become obscured and enveloped in darkness."

Counsels and Reminiscences

YOU really are a saint!" some one said to her.

"No, I am not a saint; I have never done the works of the Saints. I am a very, very little soul on whom the good God has outpoured the abundance of His grace. You will see in Heaven that I am telling you the truth."

Counsels and Reminiscences

SHE said to the Prioress: "Mother, I feel that if I were unfaithful, if I committed but the very slightest infidelity, fearful troubles would follow, and I could no longer accept death with resignation."

And as the Mother Prioress showed surprise at hearing her speak thus, she continued:

"I mean an infidelity springing from pride. For instance, if I said: 'I have acquired such or such a virtue, I am able to practise it,' or, 'O my God, I love Thee too well—Thou knowest it—to dwell on one single thought against faith,' I feel that I should forthwith be assailed by the most dangerous temptations and should certainly be overcome by them.

"To avoid this calamity I have but to say humbly from the depths of my heart: 'O my God, I implore of Thee, suffer me not to be unfaithful!'

"I very well understand how St. Peter fell. He depended too confidently on the fervor of his feelings, instead of relying solely upon Divine strength. Had he said to Jesus: 'Lord, give me the strength to follow Thee even unto death,' that strength, I am quite sure would not have been refused him."

Counsels and Reminiscences

OH! when I think of all I have to acquire!" exclaimed a novice.

"Say, rather, *to lose*. Jesus, it is, who charges Himself with the care of filling your soul according as you free it from its imperfections. I plainly see that you are taking the wrong road, you will never arrive at the end of your journey. You wish to scale a mountain and the good God wants to make you descend: He is waiting for you low down in the fertile valley of humility."

Counsels and Reminiscences

WHEN I receive a reproof," said another, "I would rather have deserved it than be wrongfully accused."

"As for me," replied Thérèse, "I prefer being blamed unjustly, then I have no cause for self-reproach and I offer this unmerited blame to the good God with joy, then I humble myself at the thought that I should be quite capable of doing that of which I was accused."

Counsels and Reminiscences

WHEN we are not understood, and are unfavorably judged, what good is there in defending ourselves? Let us leave it so and say nothing, it is so sweet to let ourselves be judged no matter how! It is not told in the Gospels that Saint Magdalen gave any explanation when blamed by her sister for sitting inactive at the feet of Jesus. She did not say: "Martha, if thou didst but know my happiness, if thou didst but hear the words I hear, thou too wouldst lay all else aside, to share my joy and my repose." No, she chose rather to be silent . . . O blessed silence which gives to the soul such peace!

Counsels and Reminiscences

IN a moment of temptation and combat a novice received this note:

"The just man shall correct me in mercy and reprove me; but let not the oil of the sinner anoint my head.[41] I cannot be corrected or tried except by the just, inasmuch as all my Sisters are pleasing to God. It is less bitter to be reproved by a sinner than by the just; but *through compassion for sinners*, to obtain their conversion, I pray Thee, O my God, that I may be bruised by the just souls who are round about me. Again, I beg that the oil of praise, so sweet to nature, *anoint not my head*, that is to say, enervate not my mind, by making me believe that I possess virtues which I have only with difficulty practised several times.

---

41 Ps., cxl, 5.

"O my Jesus! *Thy Name is as oil poured out;*[42] it is in this divine perfume that I wish to be wholly bathed, far away from the notice of creatures."

Counsels and Reminiscences

AT the close of her life she was able to say: "I used so to rise above all things, that I drew strength from humiliations."

Story of a Soul, *Ch. XII*

GOD has a special love for you," remarked a young Sister, "since to you He entrusts other souls."

"That does not add anything to me, and I am only really just what I am in God's sight . . . It does not follow that He loves me more, because He wills that I should be His interpreter to you; rather, He makes me your little servant. It is for you and not for me that He has given me the charms and virtues apparent to you.

"Often I compare myself to a little bowl which God fills with good things of every kind. All the *kittens* come to it to take their share, and sometimes there is

42 Cant., i, 2.

a contest as to which shall have most. But the Child Jesus is there, keeping watch: 'I am very willing that you drink from my little bowl' saith He, 'but take care lest you overturn it and break it.'

"Truth to tell, the danger is not great, because I am placed on the ground. It is otherwise with Prioresses: they, being set on tables run many more risks. Honors are always dangerous.

"Oh! how poisonous the praises served up day by day to those who hold high places. What baneful incense! And how necessary it is that the soul be detached from self, that so she may escape unharmed."

Counsels and Reminiscences

TO help a novice to accept a humiliation she said to her in confidence: "If I had not been received into Carmel I would have entered a Refuge, to live there unknown and despised in the midst of the poor penitents. To pass for such in the eyes of all would have been my happiness. I should have been the apostle of my companions telling them what I think of the Mercy of the good God."

"But how would you have been able to hide your innocence from your Confessor?"

"I would have told him that while in the world I had made a general confession and had been forbidden to do so again."

Counsels and Reminiscences

ONE day they brought her some ears of corn. She took one so laden with grain that it leaned down upon its stalk, and having looked at it for a long time she said to the Mother Prioress:

"Mother, this ear of corn is an image of my soul: the good God has laden me with graces for myself and for many others! . . . Oh! I wish ever to bow down beneath the abundance of Heaven's gifts, recognizing that all comes from above."

Story of a Soul, *Ch. XII*

WHAT do you think of all the graces which have been poured down upon you?

"I think that *the Spirit of God breatheth where He will.*"[43]

Counsels and Reminiscences

A SISTER said that in Heaven she would be a beautiful flower, resplendent with light.

"Oh no," she replied, "you know how in pretty bouquets they conceal some moss to make the flowers stand out; well, I shall be a little bit of moss to set off the beauty of the elect."

Counsels and Reminiscences

DURING her last agony the Mother Prioress encouraged her with these words:

"My child, you are quite ready to appear before God because you have always understood the virtue of humility."

---

[43] John, iii, 8.

Then of herself she gave this beautiful testimony:

"Yes, I feel it, my soul has never sought but the truth . . . yes, I have understood humility of heart!"

Story of a Soul, *Ch. XII*

VI
Detachment

IF the impossible were possible and that God Himself did not see my good actions, I would not grieve about it. I love Him so much that I should like to be able to give Him pleasure without His knowing that it was I . . . Knowing and seeing it, He is, in a way, bound to repay me . . . I would not give Him the trouble.

Counsels and Reminiscences

THE glory of Jesus . . . that is my whole ambition; my own I abandon to Him; and if He seem to forget me, well, He is at liberty to do so since I am mine no more, but His. He will more quickly tire of making me wait, than I, of waiting!

Letter VII to Mother Agnes of Jesus

THERE is no stay, no support to seek out of Jesus. He alone changeth not. What happiness to think that He can never change!

Letter V to Mother Agnes of Jesus

THE sole happiness upon earth consists in hiding oneself and remaining in total ignorance of created things.

Story of a Soul, *Ch. VIII*

FAR from dazzling me all the titles of nobility appear to me but empty vanity. I have understood those words of the *Imitation*: *"Be not solicitous for the shadow of a great name."*[44] I have understood that true greatness is found not in the name but in the soul.

The Prophet tells us that *the Lord God shall call His servants by ANOTHER NAME*;[45] and we read in St. John: *"To him that overcometh, I will give . . . a white counter, and in the counter a new name written, which no man knoweth but he that receiveth."*[46] It is in Heaven,

---

44 *Imit.*, III, xxiv, 2.

45 Is., lxv, 15.

46 Apoc., ii, 17.

therefore, that we shall know our titles of nobility. Then *shall each one receive from God the praise that he merits*,[47] and he who upon earth will have made choice of being the poorest and the most unknown for love of our Lord, he will be the first, the noblest and the richest.

Story of a Soul, *Ch. VI*

I THANK my Jesus for making me walk in darkness; in it I am wrapped in profound peace. Willingly I consent to stay, during the whole of my religious life, in this sombre tunnel into which He has made me enter; I desire only that my darkness may win light for sinners.

Letter IV to Mother Agnes of Jesus

IN this world we must not become attached to anything—not even things the most innocent, for they fail us at the moment when we are least expecting it. The eternal alone can satisfy us.

Letter I to Sr. Marie of the Sacred Heart

---

[47] *Cf.* I Cor., iv, 5.

THIS prayer she bore upon her heart on the day of her Profession:

"O Jesus, my Divine Spouse, grant that the robe of my baptism be never sullied! Take me, rather than suffer me here below to stain my soul by committing the slightest wilful fault. May I never seek nor ever find but Thee alone! May all creatures be nothing to me, and I nothing to them! May no earthly thing disturb my peace!

"Grant that I fulfil my engagements in all their perfection; that none concern themselves about me; that I may be trodden underfoot, forgotten, as a little grain of sand. I offer myself to Thee, O Well-Beloved, that Thou mayst ever perfectly accomplish Thy holy will in me, without let or hindrance from creatures."

Story of a Soul, *Ch. VIII*

WITH jealous care all must be kept for Jesus; it is so good to work for Him, and for Him alone! How joyous then the heart and how buoyant the spirit! . . .

Letter VI to Mother Agnes of Jesus

I HAVE never wished for human glory, contempt it was, that had attraction for my heart; but having recognized that this again was too glorious for me, I ardently desire to be forgotten.

Letter VII to Mother Agnes of Jesus

IF you only knew to what a degree I wish to be indifferent to the things of the earth! What matters to me all created beauty? I should be truly unfortunate were I to possess it. Oh! how great, how noble, seems my heart when I look at it in relation to this world's goods, since all of them put together could never satisfy it; but when I consider it with reference to Jesus, how *small* it then appears to me.

Letter II to Mother Agnes of Jesus

YES, I now am able to say I have received the grace of being no more attached to the goods of mind and heart than to those of earth. If it happens that I repeat to my Sisters some thought of mine which pleases them, I think it quite natural that they should look on it as their own; this thought belongs to the

Holy Ghost not to me, seeing that St. Paul tells us *that without the Spirit of Love we cannot give to God the name of Father.*[48] The Holy Spirit assuredly is free to use me as the means of conveying a good thought to a soul and I may not consider this thought as my property.

Story of a Soul, *Ch. X*

THERE is one only means of constraining the good God not to judge us at all, it is to appear before Him with our hands empty."

"But how?" they asked her.

"It is quite simple: keep nothing whatever in reserve, give away your gains according as you earn. As for me, if I live to be eighty I shall be always poor; I know not how to save up, all that I have goes immediately to ransom souls."

Counsels and Reminiscences

THE further you advance the fewer combats will you have, or rather, the easier will your conquests be, because you will look at the good side of things.

---

48 *Cf.* Rom., viii, 15.

Your soul will then rise above creatures. Anything that may be said to me now, leaves me absolutely indifferent, for I have realized how little stability there is in human judgments.

Counsels and Reminiscences

TO write books of devotion, to compose the most sublime poetry, is of less worth than the least act of self-renunciation.

Counsels and Reminiscences

ONE Sunday," Thérèse tells us, "I went right joyously on my way towards the alley of chestnut trees; it was the spring-time, and I meant to enjoy the beauties of nature. O cruel disappointment! My dear chestnut trees had been pruned, and the branches, already loaded with verdant buds, lay strewn upon the ground! It was heartrending to view this destruction, and to think that three years must pass ere I could see it repaired . . . My distress however did not last. 'If I were in another monastery,' thought I, 'what difference would it make to me if the chestnut trees in the Carmel of Lisieux were cut down altogether? I will fret no more about transitory things; my Well-Beloved shall take the place of all else for me . . . I will wander ever in the groves of His love, which none may touch!'"

Counsels and Reminiscences

SHE said to her novices: "You are too much taken up about what you are doing, you torment yourselves concerning the future as if you had the care of it . . . Are you at this moment preoccupied with what is passing in other Carmels, as to whether the nuns are pressed or not? Do their labors hinder your prayer or meditation? Very well, so, too, ought you to be detached from your personal work, employing conscientiously therein the time directed, but with disengagement of heart.

"I have read that the Israelites, when building the walls of Jerusalem, worked with one hand and with the other held a sword.[49] That is truly a figure of what we ought to do: never give ourselves completely up to the work."

Counsels and Reminiscences

---

[49] II Esdras, iv, 17.

A NOVICE asked some of the Sisters to help to shake blankets, which being rather worn, she cautioned them somewhat sharply to be careful not to tear. St. Thérèse remarked:

"What would you do if it were not your office to mend these blankets? . . . With what detachment you would then act! And if you did point out that they are easily torn, how free from self-interest it would be. Thus, never let the least shadow of self-interest glide into your actions."

Counsels and Reminiscences

IN the infirmary the novices used scarcely to wait till her thanksgivings were ended before speaking to her and seeking her counsels. This, at first, grieved her and she gently reproached them. Then very soon she let them have their way, saying:

"The thought has struck me that I am not to desire more of repose than our Lord. When He retired into the desert after His discourses, the people came immediately to break in upon His solitude. Come to me as much as you will. I must die arms in hand, *having on my lips the sword of the Spirit which is the Word of God.*"[50]

Counsels and Reminiscences

HOW do you manage so to practise virtue," asked a novice, "as to be always the same, invariably joyous and composed?"

"It has not been always so," she replied, "but ever since I have shunned all self-seeking I lead the happiest life that can be."

Counsels and Reminiscences

NOW, that I am about to appear before the good God, more than ever do I understand that there is but one thing necessary: to work solely for Him, and to do nothing for self or for creatures.

Letter X to her Missionary "Brothers"

[50] Ephes., vi, 17.

VII

Mortification

FAR from being like to those great souls who from their childhood practise all sorts of macerations, I made my mortification consist solely in the breaking of my will, restraining a hasty word, rendering little services to those around me without making anything of it, and a thousand other things of this kind.

Story of a Soul, *Ch. VI*

AS I had no taste for games, I should have liked to spend my life reading, but I was only to take a very limited time for this chosen recreation, and this was the ground of many a sacrifice, for I made it a point of duty to break off promptly at the end of the time allotted, even in the middle of the most interesting passage.

Story of a Soul, *Ch. IV*

I HAD accustomed myself never to complain when anything of mine was taken away; and when unjustly blamed I chose rather to remain silent than to defend myself.

Story of a Soul, *Ch. I*

I WAS ten years old the day that my Father told Celine he was going to let her have lessons in painting; I was by, and envied her. Then Papa said to me: "And you, my little queen, would it give you pleasure too to learn drawing?" I was just going to respond with a very gladsome *yes*, when Marie made the remark that I had not the same taste for it as Celine. At once she gained the day; and I, thinking that here was a good opportunity of offering a grand sacrifice to Jesus, said not a word. So eager was my desire to learn drawing that now I still wonder how I had the fortitude to remain silent.

Story of a Soul, *Ch. VIII*

IN the world, on awakening in the morning I used to think over what would probably occur either pleasing or vexatious during the day; and if I foresaw only trying events I arose dispirited. Now it is quite the other way: I think of the difficulties and the sufferings that await me, and I rise the more joyous and full of courage the more I foresee opportunities of proving my love for Jesus, and *earning the living of my children*—seeing that I am *the mother* of souls. Then I kiss my crucifix and lay it tenderly on the pillow while I dress, and I say to Him: "My Jesus, Thou hast worked enough and wept enough during the three-and-thirty years of Thy life on this poor earth. Take now Thy rest . . . My turn it is to suffer and to fight."

Counsels and Reminiscences

THE attraction to penance was given me, but I was permitted nothing to satisfy it. The only mortifications I was allowed consisted in mortifying self-love, which did me more good than corporal penance.

Story of a Soul, *Ch. VII*

AT prayer I was for a long time near a Sister who used to handle incessantly either her Rosary-beads or some other thing; perhaps none heard it but myself, for my hearing is extremely acute, but I cannot say how it tormented me! I should have liked to turn my head and look at the culprit so as to make her stop that noise: however in my heart I knew it was better to bear it patiently, for the love of God in the first place, and also to avoid giving pain.

I kept quiet therefore, but was sometimes worked up to fever-heat and obliged to make simply a prayer of endurance. Finally I sought out the means of suffering with peace and joy, at least in my innermost soul; I tried to like the teasing little noise. Instead of endeavoring not to hear it—a thing impossible—I listened with fixed attention as if it had been a delightful concert; and my prayer, *which was not the prayer of quiet*, passed in offering this concert to Jesus.

Another time I was in the laundry opposite a Sister who while washing handkerchiefs splashed me every minute with dirty water. My first impulse was to draw back and wipe my face, so as to show her who besprinkled me in that fashion, that she would oblige me by working more quietly; but I reflected immediately that it was very foolish to refuse treasures so generously offered me, and I took good care not to show my annoyance. On the contrary, I made such successful efforts to *wish* for a plentiful splashing of dirty water, that at the end of half an hour I had really acquired a taste for this new sort of aspersion, and I determined to come again as often as possible to a place where happily such riches could be had gratuitously.

Story of a Soul, *Ch. X*

I REMEMBER that sometimes, when a postulant, I was so violently tempted to indulge myself by seeking some little consolations, that I was obliged to go quickly past our Mother's cell, and cling to the banisters of the staircase so that I should not turn back. There would come to mind a number of permissions to ask, a hundred pretexts for deciding in favor of my natural inclinations and gratifying them. How glad I am now of having denied myself from the outset of my life in religion! Already I enjoy the reward promised to those who fight courageously. No longer do I feel the necessity of refusing myself consolations of the heart; for my heart is firmly fixed in God . . . Because it has loved Him above all, it has gradually enlarged, even so as to love those who are dear to it with a love incomparably deeper than if it were centered in a selfish and fruitless affection.

Story of a Soul, *Ch. X*

IN everything I must find self-denial and sacrifice; thus I feel that a letter will not bear fruit unless I write it with a certain reluctance, and solely through obedience. When conversing with a novice I am careful to mortify myself and to avoid asking her questions which would gratify my curiosity. If she commence to speak of something interesting, then, leaving it unfinished, pass to a subject wearisome to me, I take care not to remind her of the interruption, for it seems to me that one can do no good by self-seeking.

Story of a Soul, *Ch. X*

GOD did not permit that our Mother should tell me to write down my poems according as I composed them, and I would not have liked to ask her, fearing lest that might be a fault against poverty. So I used to wait until the hour of free time, and it was not without extreme difficulty that I recalled to mind, at eight o'clock in the evening, what I had composed in the morning.

These little nothings are a martyrdom it is true, but we must be well on our guard not to lessen it by allowing ourselves, or seeking to be allowed, a thousand things which would render the religious life pleasant and comfortable.

Counsels and Reminiscences

WHEN some one rings for us, or knocks at our door, we must mortify ourselves so as not even to do one stitch more before answering. I have practised that; and it is, I assure you, a source of peace.

Counsels and Reminiscences

DO you know my Sundays and festivals? They are the days when the good God tries me the most.

Counsels and Reminiscences

SAINT Thérèse of the Child Jesus says that she has not done any great penances: that is because her fervor counted as nothing those which were allowed her. It nevertheless happened that she became ill from wearing for too long a time a small iron cross, of which the sharp points were sunk into her flesh.

"That would not have befallen me from so slight a penance," she said afterwards, "if the good God had not wanted to make me understand that the macerations of the Saints are not intended for me, nor for the little souls who will tread the same path of spiritual childhood."

Story of a Soul, *Ch. XII*

TO a novice whom she saw practise a little act of self-denial she said:

"You will be very glad to find that before you at the moment of death. What you have just done is more glorious than if, by some skilful measures, you had gained for the religious communities the good-will of the Government, and that all France applauded you as a Judith."

Counsels and Reminiscences

TO another who was bewailing her want of courage: "You complain of what should cause you the greatest happiness. Where would be your merit if you must fight only when you felt the courage? What matters it if you have none, provided that you act as if you had! If you feel too slothful to pick up a bit of thread, and that nevertheless you do it for the love of Jesus, you have more merit than if in a moment of fervor you were to accomplish something of far greater importance. So instead of being sorrowful, rejoice to see that in letting you feel your weakness the good Master provides you with an opportunity of gaining for Him a greater number of souls."

Counsels and Reminiscences

BEING questioned as to her mode of sanctifying the repasts, Thérèse made answer:

"In the refectory we have but one only thing to do: to accomplish this so lowly act with thoughts uplifted. I declare to you that often it is in the refectory the sweetest aspirations of love come to me. Sometimes I am impelled to dwell on the thought that if our Divine Lord were in my place, with the fare set before Him as served to me, He would certainly partake of it . . . It is very probable that during His life on earth He tasted of the like food: *He ate bread, fruits, etc.* . . .

"Here are my simple little rubrics:

"I picture myself at Nazareth in the house of Holy Family. If I am served with, for instance, salad, cold fish, wine or anything of strong flavor, I offer it to St. Joseph. To the Blessed Virgin I give the hot portions, well-ripened fruits, etc.; and the feast-day fare, particularly corn-flour, rice, preserves, these I offer to the Child Jesus. Lastly, when a bad dinner is brought me I say gaily to myself: 'Today, my dear little child, all that is for you.'"

Counsels and Reminiscences

ONE fast-day when the Mother Prioress had ordered some special little thing by way of alleviation for St. Thérèse, a Sister relates that she surprised her in the act of seasoning this too palatable fare with wormwood.

Another time she saw her slowly drinking some particularly disagreeable physic, and exclaimed: "But be quick, drink that off at one draught!" "Oh no!" was the reply, "must I not take advantage of the trifling opportunities I meet with, to mortify myself a little, since it is forbidden me to look for greater?"

Counsels and Reminiscences

AN extremely interesting letter had been read one day at the recreation in the absence of Thérèse who later showed a desire to read it. Some time afterwards when returning the letter, she was begged to say what she thought regarding something which should especially have delighted her. She appeared embarrassed and then replied:

"The good God has asked of me this sacrifice because of the eagerness that I manifested the other day; I have not read it. . ."

Counsels and Reminiscences

SHE told the novices: "At recreation more than elsewhere will you find occasions for the exercise of virtue. If you would reap great benefit, never go to it with any thought of your own recreation, but thinking of the recreation of others; practise therein total detachment from yourself. If, for instance, you are relating to one of the Sisters a story which seems to you interesting, and that she interrupts it to tell you something else, even though this may not at all interest you, listen to her as if it did, and do not try to return to your first subject. By so acting, you will go from the recreation room with great interior peace, and endued with fresh vigor in the practice of virtue, all because you have not sought to gratify yourself but to give pleasure to others. If one only knew what is gained by renouncing self in all things! . . ."

"You know it well; you have always acted thus?"

"Yes, I have forgotten self, I have tried not to seek myself in anything."

Counsels and Reminiscences

VIII
Obedience

AS I had self-love as well as the love of what is right it was sufficient but once to tell me: "Such a thing should not be done," and I would have no desire to do it again.

Story of a Soul, *Ch. I*

FROM what anxieties do we not free ourselves by making the vow of obedience! How happy are single-minded religious. Their sole guide being the will of Superiors, they are ever secure of going the right way without fear of error, should it even appear to them certain that the Superiors are mistaken. But when one ceases to consult the sure compass, the soul forthwith loses her way in arid paths where the waters of grace soon fail her.

Story of a Soul, *Ch. IX*

DURING her illness the infirmarian had recommended St. Thérèse to take a little walk in the garden every day for a quarter of an hour. For her, this advice was a command. One afternoon, a Sister seeing her walk with much difficulty said to her: "You would do far better to rest; in such circumstances walking can do you no good, you exhaust yourself, that is all."

"It is true," replied this child of Obedience, "but do you know what gives me strength? . . . Well! *I walk for a missionary*. I think how some one of them far away, yonder, is perhaps exhausted in his apostolic journeyings, and to lessen his fatigue I offer mine to the good God."

Story of a Soul, *Ch. XII*

IX

Poverty

After I was clothed with the holy Habit abundant lights on religious perfection were granted me, chiefly regarding the vow of poverty. During my postulate I was pleased to have for my use, anything that was nice, and to find at my hand whatever was necessary. Jesus bore with this patiently, for He does not like to disclose all to the soul at once. He ordinarily gives His light little by little.

After Compline one evening I looked in vain for our lantern on the shelves appointed for them; it was the time of great silence, not possible therefore to ask for it back. I rightly supposed that a Sister believing she took her own had carried away ours; but must I spend a whole hour in the dark in consequence of this mistake? And just that evening I had intended doing much work. Without the interior light of grace I should assuredly have bewailed my loss, but with that light, instead of experiencing vexation I was happy in thinking that poverty consists in being deprived not only of things desirable, but of those also that are indispensable. And in the exterior darkness I found my soul illumined with divine light.

I was seized at this time with a genuine love for what was ugliest and least convenient, thus I was delighted when I saw the pretty little jug carried off from our cell, and received in its stead a large one, all chipped.

Story of a Soul, *Ch. VII*

A NOVICE expressed regret for having lent a pin which was very serviceable to her:

"Oh! how rich you are," replied Thérèse, "you cannot be happy."

Counsels and Reminiscences

"*MAKE haste and come down: for this day I must abide in thy house.*"[51] Jesus tells us to come down; where, then, must we go? . . . At an earlier time the Jews asked Him: *"Master, where dwellest Thou."*[52] And He

51 Luke, xix, 5

52 John, i, 38.

said: *"The foxes have holes, and the birds of the air nests; but the Son of Man hath not where to lay His head."*[53] Behold whereunto we must descend if we would serve as dwellings for Jesus: we must be so poor that we have not where to lay our head.

Letter XIII to her Sister Celine

[53] Luke, ix, 58.

X

Confidence

WHAT offends Jesus, what wounds Him to the Heart, is want of confidence.

Letter I to her Cousin Marie Guerin

BELIEVING that I was born for glory, and seeking the means to attain to it, it was revealed to me interiorly that my glory would never be visible to mortal eyes but would consist in becoming a saint. This desire might well seem presumptuously bold, considering how imperfect I was, and how imperfect I am still after so many years in religion; and yet I feel ever the same audacious confidence of becoming a great saint. I count not on my merits, having none; but I trust in Him who is Virtue and Holiness itself. He alone it is who satisfied with my feeble efforts will raise me up even unto Himself, will clothe me with His merits and make me a saint.

Story of a Soul, *Ch. IV*

OURS is an age of inventions: nowadays, with the rich a lift saves the trouble of climbing the stairs. And I, fain would I too find a *lift* to bear me up unto God, for I am too little to climb the rugged steps of perfection.

Then I turned to the Holy Scriptures, seeking from them an indication of this *lift*, the object of my desires; and I read these words which have issued from the very mouth of the Eternal Wisdom: *"Whosoever is a VERY LITTLE ONE, let him come to me."*[54] Then I drew nigh unto God divining truly that I had discovered what I sought: wishing however to know what He would do with the very little one, I continued my research and here is what I found: *"You shall be carried at the breast and upon the knees; as one whom the mother caresseth so will I comfort you."*[55]

Ah, never came words more sweet, more tender, to gladden my soul. Thine arms then, O Jesus, are the *lift* which must raise me up even unto Heaven! For this I need not grow, on the contrary I must remain little, I must ever tend to become yet more little. O my God, Thou hast gone beyond my expectations, and I—I will sing Thy mercies! *Thou hast taught me, O God from my*

54 Prov., ix, 4.

55 Is., lxvi, 12, 13.

youth: and till now I have declared Thy wondrous works. And unto old age and grey hairs[56] will I proclaim them.

Story of a Soul, *Ch. IX*

SINCE it has been given to me too, to understand the love of the Heart of Jesus, I own that it has chased all fear from mine! The remembrance of my faults humiliates me, and urges me never to depend upon my own strength which is nothing but weakness: still more does this remembrance speak to me of mercy and of love. When, with all filial confidence we cast our faults into the devouring furnace of love, how should they not be totally consumed?

Letter V to her Missionary "Brothers"

THOUGH we must needs be pure indeed to appear in the presence of the God of all Holiness, yet I know too that He is infinitely just; and this justice which affrights so many souls is the ground of my joy and my confidence. Justice not merely exercises severity towards the offender; it moreover recognizes a right

56 *Cf.* Ps., lxx. 17, 18.

intention, and awards to virtue its recompense. I hope as much from the Justice of the good God as from His Mercy; it is because He is just, that *"He is compassionate and merciful, long-suffering and plenteous in mercy. For He knoweth our frame. He remembereth that we are but dust. As a father hath compassion on His children, so hath the Lord compassion on us!"*[57] . . .

Listening to these beautiful and consoling words of the Royal Prophet, how can we doubt but that the good God will open the portals of His Kingdom to His children who have loved Him even unto sacrificing all for Him, who have not only left their kindred and their country, for the sake of making Him known and loved, but, still further, desire to give their life for Him? . . . Most truly has Jesus said that there is no greater love than this! How then could He suffer Himself to be outdone in generosity? How could He purify in the flames of Purgatory souls consumed by the fire of Divine Love? . . .

That is what I think of the justice of the good God; my way is all confidence and love, I do not understand those souls who fear so tender a Friend.

Letter VI to her Missionary "Brothers"

---

[57] Ps., cii, 8, 13, 14.

THAT joy to think that God is just, that is to say, that He takes our weakness into consideration, that He thoroughly knows the frailty of our nature. Of what then, should I be afraid? Must not the good and infinitely just God, who with such tender mercy deigns to pardon the Prodigal Son, must He not be just towards me too—*who am always with Him?*[58]

Story of a Soul, *Ch. VIII*

I WANT to make you understand by a very simple comparison how much Jesus loves souls, even the imperfect, who trust in Him. Suppose the father of two wayward and disobedient children, coming to punish them, sees one tremble and draw away from him in terror; while the other, on the contrary, throwing himself into his arms, says he is sorry, promises to be good henceforward and begs for a kiss as punishment. Do you think the delighted father will withstand the filial confidence of this child? He knows nevertheless that his son will fall again many a time into the same faults, but he is disposed to pardon him always, if always there be an appeal to his heart.

---

[58] Luke, xv, 31.

I say nothing of the other child: you must understand that his father cannot love him as much or treat him with the same indulgence.

Letter VIII to her Missionary "Brothers"

TRULY the Heart of Jesus is more grieved by the thousand little imperfections of His friends than by even grave faults of His enemies. But it seems to me that it is only when His own chosen ones make a habit of these infidelities, and do not ask His pardon, that He can say: *"These wounds which you see in the midst of My Hands: with these was I wounded in the house of them that loved Me."*[59]

For those who love Him and who come after each little fault and throw themselves into His arms, begging His forgiveness, the Heart of Jesus thrills with joy. He says to His Angels what the father of the prodigal son said to His servants: *"Put a ring on his finger and let us rejoice."*[60] Oh! the goodness and the merciful love of the Heart of Jesus, how little is it known! True it is, that to share in these treasures we must humble ourselves,

---

59 *Cf.* Zach., xiii, 6.
60 *Cf.* Luke, xv, 22.

must acknowledge our nothingness, and that is what many souls are unwilling to do.

Letter VII to her Missionary "Brothers"

OUR dreams, our desires of perfection are not vain imaginations, since Jesus Himself has given us this commandment, He said: *"Be you, therefore, perfect, as also your Heavenly Father is perfect."*[61]

Letter II to her Sister Celine

TRULY I am far from being a saint. I ought not to rejoice at the aridity of my soul, but attribute it to the scantiness of my fervor and fidelity. I ought to grieve because I fall asleep very often during my prayer and my thanksgiving. Well, I do not grieve! I reflect that little children when they sleep are as pleasing to their parents as when they are awake; that in order to perform operations, doctors put their patients to sleep; in fine, that *the Lord knoweth our frame, He remembereth that we are but dust.*[62]

Story of a Soul, *Ch. VIII*

---

61 Matt., v, 48.

62 Ps., cii, 14.

I HAVE no fear of the last combats, nor of the physical suffering how great soever it may be. The good God has always come to my assistance, He has helped me and led me by the hand from my earliest years . . . I count on Him . . . my sufferings may reach their furthest limits, but I am sure that He will never abandon me.

Story of a Soul, *Ch. XII*

IT is confidence, and confidence alone, that must lead us to Love . . . Does not fear lead us rather to think of the rigid justice by which sinners are warned? But that is not the justice that Jesus will show to those who love Him.

Letter VI to Sister Marie of the Sacred Heart

O JESUS, suffer me to tell Thee that Thy Love reacheth even unto folly . . . What wilt Thou, in face of this folly, but that my heart dart upwards to Thee—how can my confidence have any bounds?

Story of a Soul, *Ch. XI*

IT is not because I have been shielded from mortal sin that I lift up my heart to God in trust and love. I feel that even if there lay upon my conscience all the crimes one could commit I should lose nothing of my confidence. Brokenhearted with compunction I would go and throw myself into the arms of my Saviour. I know that He cherished the Prodigal Son, I have heard His words to Mary Magdalene, to the adultress, to the Samaritan woman. No one could frighten me, for I know what to believe concerning His Mercy and His Love. I know that in one moment all that multitude of sins would disappear—as a drop of water cast into a red-hot furnace.

It is related in the Lives of the Fathers of the Desert that one of them converted a public sinner whose misdeeds scandalized the whole country. Touched by grace this sinful woman was following the saint into the desert, there to do rigorous penance, when, on the first night of her journey, before she had even reached the place of her retreat, the bonds of life were broken by the impetuosity of her loving contrition. The holy hermit at the same moment saw her soul borne by Angels into the Bosom of God.

That is truly a striking instance of what I want to express, but one cannot put these things into words. . .

Story of a Soul, *Ch. XI*

HAPPY indeed am I to die and go to Heaven, but when I think on those words of our Lord: *"Behold, I come quickly, and My reward is with Me, to render to every man according to his works,"*[63] I reflect that He will be very much embarrassed as regards me: I have no works . . . Well, He will render to me ACCORDING TO HIS OWN WORKS!

Counsels and Reminiscences

ONE evening as they were telling her something which had been said at recreation, touching the responsibility of those who have the charge of souls, St. Thérèse of the Child Jesus spoke these beautiful words: *"'To him that is little, mercy is granted.'*[64] It is possible to remain *little*, even in the most important offices; and is it not written that at the end *the Lord will arise to save the meek and humble of the earth?*[65] It says not to *judge* but to *save*."

Story of a Soul, *Ch. XII*

---

[63] Apoc., xxii, 12.

[64] Wisdom, vi, 7.

[65] *Cf.* Ps., lxxv, 10.

A NOVICE questioning as to whether our Lord were not dissatisfied with her on account of her many miseries, Saint Thérèse made answer:

"Set your mind at rest: He whom you have chosen as your Spouse possesses certainly every perfection that can be desired; but, if I may dare to say it, He has at the same time one great infirmity: *He is blind!* And there is a science which He knows not, that of *calculation*. These two points which would be most lamentable deficiencies in an earthly spouse, render ours infinitely lovable. Were He to consider our sins and reckon with them, do you not think that in the face of all these sins He would cast us back into nothingness? But no, His love for us makes Him absolutely blind!

"See for yourself: if the greatest sinner on earth, at the hour of death repent of his transgressions and expire in an act of love, immediately, without calculating on the one hand the numerous graces abused by this unhappy man, nor on the other, all his crimes, Jesus sees nothing, counts nothing, but the penitent's last prayer, and delays not to receive him into the arms of His Mercy.

"But to render Him thus blind, to hinder Him from doing the least little bit of reckoning, we must know how to lay siege to His Heart; at that point He is defenseless. . ."

Counsels and Reminiscences

TO another, who bitterly repented of a fault just committed, St. Thérèse said:

"Take your Crucifix and kiss it."

The novice kissed the feet.

"Is that how a child embraces her Father? Put your arms round His Neck immediately and kiss His Face."

She obeyed.

"That is not all, He must return your caresses."

And she had to hold the Crucifix to each cheek; then Thérèse said:

"That is well, now all is forgiven!"

Counsels and Reminiscences

HAVING caused her pain, a novice went to ask pardon of Saint Thérèse, who replied with emotion: "If you only knew what I feel! Never have I so well understood with what love Jesus receives us, when, after a fault we beg Him to forgive us. If I, His poor little creature, feel such tenderness for you the moment you return to me, what must pass in the Heart of the good God when we return to Him? . . . Yes, surely, more swiftly yet than I have just done, will He forget all our iniquities, never again to remember them . . . He will do even more—He will love us still better than before our fault! . . ."

Counsels and Reminiscences

XI

Self-Abandonment

I CANNOT think without rapture of the dear little Saint Cecilia: what a model! In the midst of a pagan world, in the heart of danger, at the moment when about to be united to a mortal who sought none but earthly love, it seems to me that she ought to have trembled and wept. But no, *while her bridal was celebrated with joyful melody Cecilia was singing in her heart.*[66] What abandonment to God! Without doubt she listened to other melodies than those of earth; her Divine Spouse, He too, was singing, and Angel choirs sang again the refrain of one most blessed night: *"Glory to God in the highest and on earth peace to men of good will."*[67]

The glory of God!—Oh! Cecilia understood it; most earnestly did she long for it. She divined that her Jesus was athirst for souls . . . that is why her whole

---

66 Office of St. Cecilia.

67 Luke, ii, 14.

desire was that she might lead speedily to Him the soul of the young Roman, who dreamed of naught but human glory: this wise Virgin will make of him a martyr, and multitudes will follow in his footprints. She fears nothing: the Angels have promised and have sung of peace. She knows that the Prince of Peace is bound to protect her, to shield her virginity and to give to her its recompense. *"O how beautiful is the chaste generation!"*[68]

Letter XVII to her Sister Celine

I HAD offered myself to the Child Jesus to be *His little plaything.* I had told Him not to use me like a costly toy which children are pleased to look at without daring to touch; but as He would a little ball of no value, that He might throw to the ground, toss about, pierce, leave in a corner, or else press to His Heart if so it pleased Him. In a word *I wanted to amuse the little Jesus, and to give myself up to all His childlike fancies.*

Story of a Soul, *Ch. VI*

---

[68] Wisdom, iv, I.

MY heart is entirely filled with the will of Jesus; therefore when anything over and above falls to its share, this does not penetrate to its depths; it is a mere nothing which easily glides by, as oil on the surface of limpid water. Ah! if my heart were not filled up beforehand, had it to be filled by the sentiments of joy or of sadness which so quickly succeed each other, bitter indeed would be this flood-tide of pain; but these rapid alternations do no more than ruffle the surface of my soul, and I remain ever in a profound peace that nothing can disturb.

Story of a Soul, *Ch. XII*

I AM not always faithful, but I am never discouraged; I leave myself wholly in the arms of our Divine Lord; He teaches me to *draw profit from all—both good and ill that He finds in me.*[69] He teaches me to speculate in the Bank of Love, or rather it is He who acts for me without telling me how He goes to work, that is His affair and not mine; my part is complete surrender, reserving nothing to myself, not even the gratification of knowing how my credit stands with the Bank.

Letter XVI to her Sister Celine

---

[69] St. John of the Cross.

A SISTER told St. Thérèse of the strange phenomena produced by magnetism on persons who really wish to yield up their will to the mesmerizer. These details appeared to interest her keenly and on the morrow she said to the Sister:

"Your conversation yesterday did me so much good. Oh! how I wish to be magnetized by our Lord. It was my first thought on awakening. With what delight have I delivered my will up to Him. Yes, I want Him to make Himself master of my faculties in such sort that my actions shall no longer be human or personal, but wholly divine, inspired and directed by the Spirit of Love."

Counsels and Reminiscences

YOU are quite wrong to think of sorrows that the future may bring; it is, as it were, intermeddling with Divine Providence. We who run in the way of Love must never torment ourselves about anything. If I did not suffer minute by minute, it would be impossible for me to be patient; but I see only the present moment, I forget the past and I take good care not to anticipate the future. If we grow disheartened, if sometimes we despair, it is because we have been dwelling on the past or the future.

Story of a Soul, *Ch. XII*

I NO longer thirst for either suffering or death, yet both I dearly prize. Long did I call upon them as the harbingers of joy . . . Suffering has in very truth been mine, and I have thought I well nigh touched the eternal shore! I have believed from my earliest youth that *the little flower* would be gathered in its springtime; now, it is the spirit of self-abandonment alone that guides me, no other compass have I. I know not now, how to ask anything eagerly, save the perfect accomplishment of God's designs upon my soul.

Story of a Soul, *Ch. VIII*

PRAY for me," she would often say, "when I implore Heaven to come to my aid, then it is that I feel most forsaken."

"And in this desolation how do you avoid discouragement?" they asked her.

"I turn to the good God, to all the Saints, and I thank them just the same. I think they wish to see to what point I shall carry my trust . . . But not in vain have these words of Job sunk into my heart: *'Though He should kill me yet will I trust in Him.'*[70] I acknowledge it was long before I reached this degree of abandonment; our Lord has taken me and placed me there!"

Story of a Soul, *Ch. XII*

IT seems to me that nothing now hinders me from taking flight, for I no longer have any great desires, save to love, even unto dying of love. I am free, I have no fear, not even of what I most dreaded; I mean the fear of being a long time ill and consequently a burthen to the Community. If it gives pleasure to the good God I willingly consent to see my life of suffering, both of soul and body, prolonged for years. Oh! no, I do not fear a long life. I do not shun the combat. *"The Lord is the rock upon which I am founded. Who teacheth my hands to fight and my fingers to war; He is my protector in whom I have hoped."*[71] Never have I asked God to

[70] Job, xiii, 15.

[71] *Cf.* Ps., cxliii, 1, 2, 3.

let me die young; it is true I have ever believed that it would be so, but without seeking to obtain it.

Story of a Soul, *Ch. IX*

WHATEVER the good God has given me has always pleased me, even the gifts which have appeared to me less good and less beautiful than those received by others.

Counsels and Reminiscences

I HAVE no greater desire to die than to live; if our Lord gave me the choice I would choose nothing; I only will what He wills; it is what He does that I love.

Story of a Soul, *Ch. XII*

SOME think you are afraid of death," they said to her.—"That may indeed yet happen; I never depend on my own thoughts, knowing how weak I am; but at present I will rejoice in the sentiments that the good God now gives me, there will be time enough to suffer from the contrary."

Story of a Soul, *Ch. XII*

A SISTER said to her:

"If anyone goes straight to Heaven, you surely will not spend one moment in Purgatory!"

"Oh! I feel little anxiety about that; I shall always be content with the sentence of the good God. If I go to Purgatory, well—I shall walk in the midst of the flames, like the three Hebrews in the furnace, singing the Canticle of Love."

Counsels and Reminiscences

XII

Gratitude

OH, how happy God makes me! How easy and how sweet it is to serve Him upon earth.

Story of a Soul, *Ch. X*

SEEING several of my companions form special attachments to some one or other of our mistresses, I wished to follow their example but could not succeed therein. O happy inability! from how great evils has it saved me . . . How I thank God for having made me find only bitterness in the friendships of earth. With a heart such as mine I should have been captured and had my wings clipped; then how should I have been able to *fly away and be at rest.*[72]

Story of a Soul, *Ch. IV*

---

[72] Ps., liv, 7.

I UNDERSTAND well that our Lord knew I was too weak to be exposed to temptation; without doubt I should have been wholly destroyed had I been dazzled by the deceitful glamour of the love of creatures; but never has it shone before my eyes. There, where strong souls find joy, and through fidelity detach themselves from it, I have found only affliction. Where then is my merit in not being given up to these fragile attachments, since it is only by a gracious effect of God's mercy that I was preserved from it? Without Him, I recognize that I might have fallen as low as St. Magdalene; and that word of deep meaning spoken by the Divine Master to Simon the Pharisee, re-echoes with great sweetness in my soul. Yes, I know it: *"To whom less is forgiven, he loveth less."*[73] But I also know that Jesus has forgiven more to me than to St. Magdalene. Ah, how I wish I could express what I feel. Here at least is an example which will in some measure convey my thought.

Suppose the son of a skilful doctor is tripped by a stone in his path, which causes him to fall and fracture a limb. His father comes in haste, lifts him up lovingly and attends to his injuries, employing therein all the resources of his art; and the boy, very soon completely

---

[73] Luke, vii, 47.

cured, testifies his gratitude. This child has certainly good reason to love so kind a father; but here is another supposition.

The father having learnt that there lies in his son's way a dangerous stone, sets out beforehand and removes it unseen by anyone. His son, the object of this tender forethought, unaware of the misfortune from which he has been preserved by the father's hand, will of course show no gratitude, and will love him less than if he had cured him of a grievous wound. But should he come to know all, will he not love him still more? Well—I am this child, the object of the preventing love of a Father *Who sent His Son not to redeem the just but sinners.*[74] He wills that I should love Him because He has forgiven me, not *much*, but *everything*. Without waiting for me to love Him much, like St. Mary Magdalene, He has made me to know how He had loved me with a preventing and ineffable love, in order that I may now love Him even unto folly!

Story of a Soul, *Ch. IV*

---

[74] Luke, v, 32.

WALKING one day in the garden, leaning on one of her sisters, Thérèse paused to enjoy the fascinating sight of a little white hen sheltering its chickens beneath its wings. Very soon her eyes filled with tears, and turning to her dear companion she said: "I can stay no longer, let us go in again quickly. . ." And in her cell, her tears continued falling and she could not utter a word. At last, looking at her sister with an expression that was quite heavenly, she said:

"I was thinking of our Lord, and of the touching comparison He chose in order to make us believe in His tenderness. That is just what He has done for me all my life: *He has wholly hidden me beneath His wings!* I cannot express what passed within my heart. Ah! the good God does well to veil Himself from my sight, to show me the effects of His Mercy rarely, and as it were, *'through the lattices;'*[75] such consolations would, I feel, be more than I could bear."

Story of a Soul, *Ch. XII*

[75] Cant., ii, 9.

OH! how *good* is the good God!" . . . she would sometimes exclaim. "Yes, He must indeed be good to give me the strength to endure all that I suffer."

Story of a Soul, *Ch. XII*

ONE day she said to the Mother Prioress: "I would like to speak to you, Mother, of the state of my soul; but I cannot, I am too deeply moved just now."

And in the evening she sent these lines pencilled with a trembling hand:

"O my God, how good Thou art to the little victim of Thy Merciful Love! Now even though Thou dost join physical suffering to the trials of my soul, I cannot say: '*The sorrows of death have encompassed me.*'[76] But I cry out in my gratitude: '*I have gone down into the valley of the shadow of death, yet I fear no evil, because Thou, O Lord, art with me.*'"[77]

Story of a Soul, *Ch. XII*

---

76 Ps., xvii, 5.

77 *Cf.* Ps., xxii, 4.

XIII
Zeal

THE cry of Jesus agonizing, "I thirst!" reechoed continually in my heart, firing it with an ardent zeal till then unknown to me. I longed to give to my Beloved to drink: I too felt myself consumed with the thirst for souls, and at all cost I would wrest sinners from the eternal flames.

Story of a Soul, *Ch. V*

THE Precious Blood of Jesus I poured on souls, to Him I offered these same souls renewed by the Dew of Calvary; thus I thought to quench His Thirst; but the more I gave Him to drink, the more ardently my poor little soul thirsted—and this I received as a most precious recompense.

Story of a Soul, *Ch. V*

LIKE the Prophets and the Doctors I would fain enlighten souls. Fain would I travel the earth, O my Well-Beloved, to preach Thy Name and to set up Thy glorious Cross in Pagan lands. But one mission only would not suffice for me; would that I could at one and the same time proclaim the Gospel all the world over, even to the remotest of its islands. I would desire to be a Missionary not only for a few years, but to have been one from the creation of the world, and so to continue to the end of time.

Story of a Soul, *Ch. XI*

I LONG to accomplish the most heroic deeds. I feel within me the courage of a Crusader. I would die on the battlefield in defense of the Church.

Story of a Soul, *Ch. XI*

OPEN, my Jesus, thy Book of Life wherein are recorded the actions of all the Saints; those actions—would that I too, had accomplished such for Thee!

Story of a Soul, *Ch. XI*

SOULS—dear Lord, we must have souls! Above all, souls of apostles and of martyrs, that through them we may inflame the multitude of poor sinners with love of Thee.

Story of a Soul, *Appendix*

AFTER recreation one day when the Mother Prioress had spoken of the persecution already raging against Religious Communities, St. Thérèse said to a novice: "Ah! Sister, we live in an era of martyrs! Blood will be shed.—What happiness if it should be ours!"

Counsels and Reminiscences

A NOVICE on her way to the laundry one day, went at a slow pace through the garden, looking at the flowers as she passed. Saint Thérèse who followed walking quickly, soon overtook her and said: "Is that how one hastens who has children (*souls*) to support, for whose sustenance she is obliged to work? . . . "

Counsels and Reminiscences

DURING her illness she wrote:

"The will of the good God is my sole desire; and I declare that if in Heaven I could no longer work for His glory, I would choose exile rather than the Fatherland."

Letter IV to her Missionary "Brothers"

WHAT draws me towards the Heavenly Country is the call of our Lord, the hope of at last loving Him as I have so ardently desired, and the thought that I shall be able to make Him loved by *a multitude of souls* who will bless Him eternally.

Letter VIII to her Missionary "Brothers"

CONFIDENTLY I count upon not remaining inactive in Heaven, my desire is to work still for the Church and for souls: this I ask of God, and I am certain that He will hear me. If I quit already the battlefield, it is not with the selfish desire of taking my rest. Suffering has long since become my heaven here below, and it is difficult to imagine how it will be possible for me to become acclimatized to a country where joy reigns, unmingled with sorrow. Jesus must needs transform my soul completely, else I could not support eternal bliss.

Story of a Soul, *Ch. XII*

JUST now a few notes of distant music fell upon my ear, and set me thinking that very soon I shall hear melodies beyond compare; yet this thought can give me but a moment's gladness; one only expectation makes my heart throb: *it is the love that I shall receive and the love that I shall be able to give!*

I feel that my mission is now to begin, my mission to make others love the good God as I love Him . . . to give to souls my little way. I WILL SPEND MY HEAVEN IN DOING GOOD UPON EARTH. This is not impossible, since the Angels in the full enjoyment of the Beatific Vision keep watch over us. No, I shall never rest till the end of the world! But when the Angel shall have said: "Time is no more!"[78] then I shall rest—shall be able to rejoice, because the number of the elect will be complete.

Story of a Soul, *Ch. XII*

---

[78] Apoc., x, 6.

XIV

Simplicity

WHEN I read certain treatises where perfection is set forth as encompassed by a thousand obstacles, my poor little head grows weary very quickly. I close the learned book which puzzles my brains and dries up my heart, and in its stead I open the Holy Scriptures. Then all appears clear, luminous . . . one single word discloses to my soul infinite horizons, perfection seems easy. I see that it is sufficient to recognize our nothingness, and to leave oneself like a child, in the arms of the good God. Let great souls and sublime intellects enjoy the beautiful books which I cannot understand, still less put in practice; I rejoice in being little, since *"children only and those who resemble them will be admitted to the Heavenly banquet."*[79]

It is well that the Kingdom of Heaven contains many mansions, for if there were none other than those of which the description and the way seem

[79] *Cf.* Matt., xix, 14.

incomprehensible to me, I should never be able to enter therein.

Letter VI to her Missionary "Brothers"

MY patrons in Heaven and my chosen favorites are those who have stolen it—like the Holy Innocents and the Good Thief. The great Saints have earned it by their works; as for me, I will imitate the thieves, I will have it by ruse, a ruse of Love which will open its gates to me and to poor sinners. The Holy Ghost encourages me, saying in the Book of Proverbs: *"O little one, come, learn subtlety of me."*[80]

Counsels and Reminiscences

OUR Lord replied to the mother of the sons of Zebedee: *"To sit on My right and on My left hand is for them for whom it is prepared by My Father."*[81] I imagine that those places of choice, refused to great Saints, to Martyrs, will be the portion of little children.

---

80 *Cf.* Prov., i, 4.

81 *Cf.* Matt., xx, 23.

Did not David predict it when he said that *the little Benjamin will preside amidst the assemblies* (of the saints)?[82]

Counsels and Reminiscences

IF you could begin your religious life over again" asked a novice, "what would you do?"

"It seems to me that I would do as I have done."

"You do not then feel like the hermit who used to say: 'Even though I had lived long years in penance yet I should fear damnation while there still remained to me one quarter of an hour, one breath of life.'

"No, I cannot share that fear, I am too little to be damned, little children are not damned."

"You always seek to be like the little ones—but tell us what we must do to possess the spirit of childhood? What does it exactly mean—to remain little?

"To remain little—it is to recognize our nothingness, to expect everything from the good God, not to be too much afflicted about our faults, for little children fall often but are too small to hurt themselves much: in fine, it is *not* to make one's fortune, nor to be disquieted

---

82 *Cf.* Ps., lxvii, 29.

about anything. Even in the homes of the poor, as long as a child is quite little they give him what is needful; but when grown up, the father is no longer willing to support him and says: 'Now work! you can provide for yourself.' Well, it was to escape hearing that, that I have never wished to grow up, for I know myself incapable of earning my livelihood—Eternal Life!

"Again, to remain little is not to attribute to self the virtues we practise; but to acknowledge that the good God places this treasure in the hand of His little child to be made use of when required."

Counsels and Reminiscences

BE not afraid to tell Jesus that you love Him; even though it be without feeling, this is the way to oblige Him to help you, and carry you like a little child too feeble to walk.

Counsels and Reminiscences

IT is a great trial to see only the black side of things, but that does not depend completely upon you. Do your best to detach your heart from the cares of this world, and above all from creatures; then you may be sure that Jesus will do the rest. He could not suffer you to fall into the abyss. Be comforted, little one, in Heaven you will no longer see *all black but all white;* yes, all will be clothed with the divine whiteness of our Spouse, the Lily of the Valley. Together we shall follow Him whithersoever He goeth . . . Oh! let us profit by the brief moments of this life to give pleasure to Jesus, let us win souls for Him by our sacrifices. Above all let us be little, so little that all the world may trample us under foot without even our appearing to feel it or to suffer from it.

Counsels and Reminiscences

YOU are wrong to find fault with one thing and another, and to seek that all should yield to your way of viewing things. We want to be like little children, and little children know not what is best, to them all seems well; let us imitate them. Besides there would be no merit [in obedience] were we only to do what would appear reasonable to us.

Counsels and Reminiscences

A NOVICE under a temptation which seemed to her insurmountable said: "This time I cannot rise above it—it is impossible." Thérèse replied: "Why do you try to rise above it? Pass beneath it quite simply. It is very well for great souls to soar high above the clouds when the storm is raging, but for us, we have merely to bear the showers with patience. If we do get rather wet—no matter! We shall dry ourselves afterwards in the sunshine of Love.

"That brings to mind this little trait of my childhood; a horse one day standing at the garden gate barred our entrance; those with me endeavored by force of talking, etc., to get him to move back, but while they talked I very quietly slipped in, through the horse's legs . . . See how one may gain by remaining little!"

Counsels and Reminiscences

TO a young Sister discouraged at seeing her imperfections, Saint Thérèse said: "You make me think of a very little child who is just able to stand upright but does not yet know how to walk. Intent upon reaching the top of the stairs so as to get back to his mother he lifts his foot to climb the first step. Fruitless endeavor! At each attempt he falls without advancing in the least. Well, be like that little child; by the practice of every virtue keep on ever lifting your little foot to climb the steps of sanctity, and do not imagine that you will be able to mount even the first! No; but good will is all God requires of you. From the top of those steps He is watching you with love; and won by your unavailing efforts He will Himself soon come down, and taking you in His arms will bear you away to His Kingdom, never more to quit Him. But if you cease to lift your little foot He will leave you a long time on earth."

Counsels and Reminiscences

THE only means of making rapid progress in the path of Love is to remain always very *little*; that is what I have done; so now I can sing with our Father St. John of the Cross:

And stooping so low, so low,
I rose still higher and higher
And thus I attained my end.

Counsels and Reminiscences

SOME one was speaking to her of the mortifications of the Saints, she replied:

"It is well our Lord has let us know that *there are many mansions in His Father's House, that if not He would have told us.*[83] Yes, if all souls called to perfection had been obliged to practise these macerations in order to enter Heaven, He would have said so, and gladly would we have undertaken them. But He tells us that *in His House there are many mansions.* If there are those for great souls, for the Fathers of the Desert and for martyrs of penance, there must be one also for little children. Our place is reserved there, if our love be great—for Him and for our Heavenly Father and the Spirit of Love."

Counsels and Reminiscences

I FEEL that my mission is now to begin," she said a few days before her death, "my mission to make others love the good God *as I love Him*, to give my *little way* to souls. . ."

"What is this 'little way' that you want to teach to souls?"

---

[83] *Cf.* John, xiv, 2.

"It is the path of spiritual childhood, it is the way of trust and of entire self-surrender. I want to make known to them the simple means that have so perfectly succeeded for me, to tell them that there is but one only thing to do here below: *to cast down before Jesus the flowers of little sacrifices, to win Him by caresses!* That is how I have won Him, and that is why I shall be so well received."

Story of a Soul, *Ch. XII*

IF I am misguiding you by my *little way* of Love, she said to a novice, do not fear that I shall let you follow it very long. I shall appear to you, and tell you to take another path; but if I do not return, believe in the truth of my words: *never can we have too much confidence in the good God, so mighty and so merciful! As much as we hope for shall we obtain from Him!* . . .

Story of a Soul, *Ch. XII*

A NOVICE said to her on the eve of the Feast of Our Lady of Mount Carmel: "If you were to die to-morrow after Holy Communion, it seems to me that so beautiful a death would console me in the midst of my grief."

And Thérèse replied with animation:

"Die after Holy Communion! On a grand Feast day! No, it will not be so: little souls could not copy that. In my little way there are only quite ordinary things; all that I do, little souls must be able to do also."

Story of a Soul, *Ch. XII*

XV
Prayer

AS I grew older I loved the good God more and more, and very frequently did I offer Him my heart, using the words my mother had taught me. I strove in all my actions to please Jesus and was most watchful never to offend Him.

Story of a Soul, *Ch. II*

MY whole strength lies in prayer and sacrifice, these are my invincible arms; they can move hearts far better than words, I know it by experience.

Story of a Soul, *Ch. X*

GREAT is the power of prayer—a queen, as one might say, having free access always to the King, and able to obtain whatever she asks. In order to be heard, it is not necessary to read from a book a beautiful form of prayer adapted to the circumstances; if it were so, how greatly to be pitied should I be!

Story of a Soul, *Ch. X*

I HAVE not the courage to force myself to seek beautiful prayers in books; not knowing which to choose I act as children do who cannot read; I say quite simply to the good God what I want to tell Him, and He always understands me.

Story of a Soul, *Ch. X*

PRAYER is, for me, an outburst from the heart; it is a simple glance darted upwards to Heaven; it is a cry of gratitude and of love in the midst of trial as in the midst of joy! In a word, it is something exalted, supernatural, which dilates the soul and unites it to God. Sometimes when I find myself, spiritually, in dryness so great that I cannot produce a single good thought, I recite very slowly a *Pater* or an *Ave Maria*; these prayers alone console me, they suffice, they nourish my soul.

Story of a Soul, *Ch. X*

THE principal plenary indulgence and one which all may gain without the ordinary conditions, is that of *charity which covereth a multitude of sins.*[84]

Counsels and Reminiscences

FORMERLY if any of my family were in trouble, and that I had been unable to succeed in comforting them during their visit, I would go from the parlour heart-broken; but soon Jesus made me understand that I was incapable of giving consolation to a soul. From that day forth I grieved no more when anyone went away sad; I confided to the good God the sorrows of those who were dear to me, feeling certain that He heard me, and at their next visit I used to find that it had indeed been so. Since I have experienced this, I no longer torment myself when involuntarily I give pain; I simply beg of Jesus to make up for what I have done.

Counsels and Reminiscences

ONE day after Holy Communion the good God made me understand those words of the

84 Prov., x, 12.

Canticles: *"Draw me: we will run offer Thee to the odor of Thy ointments."*[85] O Jesus, it is not then necessary to say: In drawing me, draw the souls whom I love. These, simple words: *"Draw me"* suffice! Yes, when a soul has allowed herself to be captivated by the inebriating fragrance of Thy perfumes, she could not run alone, all the souls whom she loves are drawn after her; this is a natural consequence of her attraction towards Thee.

Story of a Soul, *Ch. XI*

DRAW me, we will run. . ."

To ask to be drawn is to will intimate union with the object which holds the heart captive. If fire and iron were gifted with reason, and that the latter said to the fire: "Draw me," would not this prove that it desired to become identified with the fire even so far as to share its substance? Well, that is exactly my prayer. I beg of Jesus to draw me into the flames of His Love, to unite me so closely to Himself that He may live and act in me. I feel that the more the fire of love inflames my heart, the more I shall say: "Draw me," the more also

[85] Cant., i, 3.

will the souls who draw near to mine run swiftly in the fragrant odors of the Well-Beloved.

Story of a Soul, *Ch. XI*

SOULS thus on fire cannot rest inactive. They may sit at the feet of Jesus, like Saint Mary Magdalene, listening to His sweet and ardent words; but, while seeming to give nothing, they do give far more than Martha who troubles herself with *many things*.[86] It is not however of Martha's labors that Jesus disapproves, but only her too great anxiety; to this very same work His Blessed Mother humbly submitted herself, when she had to prepare the repasts for the Holy Family.

All the Saints have understood this, and more especially perhaps those who have enlightened the world with the luminous teaching of the Gospel. Was it not from prayer that Saint Paul, Saint Augustine, Saint Thomas of Aquin, Saint John of the Cross, Saint Teresa and so many other friends of God drew that wondrous science which enraptures the greatest intellects?

Archimedes said: "Give me a lever and a fulcrum, and I will raise the world." What he was unable to

---

86 Luke, x, 41

obtain because his request had but a material end and was not addressed to God, the Saints have obtained in full measure. For fulcrum, the Almighty has given them Himself, Himself alone! for lever, prayer, which enkindles the fire of love; and thus it is that they have uplifted the world, thus it is that saints still militant, uplift it, and will uplift it till the end of time.

Story of a Soul, *Ch. XI*

THE Creator of the universe awaits the prayer of one poor little soul to save a multitude of others, redeemed like her at the price of His Blood.

Our vocation is not to go and reap in the Father's fields; Jesus does not say to us: "Cast down your eyes and reap the harvest"; our mission is still more sublime. Here are the words of the Divine Master: *"Lift up your eyes and see. . ."* see that in Heaven there are empty places; yours it is to fill them . . . you are as Moses praying on the mountain; ask of Me laborers and I will send them, I await but a prayer, a sigh from out your heart!

Is not the apostolate of prayer higher as one might say, than that of preaching? It is for us to form laborers who by preaching the Gospel, will save thousands of souls of whom we thus become the mothers; what then have we to envy the Priests of the Lord?

Letter XII to her Sister Celine

HOW beautiful is our vocation! It is for us, it is for Carmel to preserve *"the salt of the earth."*[87] We offer our prayers and sacrifices for the apostles of the Lord; we ought ourselves to be their apostles while by word and example they preach the Gospel to our brethren.

Story of a Soul, *Ch. VI*

A NOVICE was grieving about her numerous distractions during prayer: "I too, have many," replied St. Thérèse of the Child Jesus, "but I accept all for love of the good God, even the most extravagant thoughts that come into my head."

Counsels and Reminiscences

[87] Matt., v, 13.

HER prayer was continual though she was habitually plunged in aridity. One day a novice entering her cell, paused, struck by the celestial expression of her countenance. She was sewing with alacrity yet seemed lost in profound contemplation.

"Of what are you thinking?" asked the young Sister. "I am meditating on the *Pater*," she replied. "It is so sweet to call the good God our Father." And tears shone in her eyes.

Story of a Soul, *Ch. XII*

I DO not well see what more I shall have in Heaven than now, she once said. I shall see the good God, it is true; but as to being with Him, I am wholly with Him already upon earth.

Story of a Soul, *Ch. XII*

A LIVING flame of Divine Love consumed her.

"A few days after my oblation to *God's Merciful Love*," she relates, "I had commenced in the Choir the Way of the Cross, when I felt myself suddenly wounded by a dart of fire so ardent that I thought I must die. I know not how to describe this transport; there is no comparison which would make one understand the intensity of that flame. An invisible power seemed to plunge me wholly into fire . . . but oh! what fire! what sweetness!"

The Mother Prioress asked her whether this transport was the first in her life, she answered simply:

"Mother, I have several times had transports of love; once especially during my novitiate when I remained one entire week far indeed from this world; for me, there was as it were, a veil thrown over all things of the earth. But I was not consumed by a real flame, I was able to sustain those delights without expecting that their intensity would cause my earthly fetters to snap asunder, whilst on the day of which I speak, one minute, one second more and my soul must have left its prison . . . Alas!—and I found myself again on earth, and aridity immediately returned to my heart!"

Story of a Soul, *Ch. XII*

XVI
Holy Communion

HOW sweet it was, the first kiss of Jesus to my soul! Yes, it was a kiss of Love. I felt I was loved, and I too said: "I love Thee, I give myself to Thee forever!" Jesus asked nothing of me, demanded no sacrifice. Already for a long time past, He and the little Thérèse had watched and understood one another . . . That day our meeting was no longer a simple look but a *fusion*. No longer were we two: Thérèse had disappeared as the drop of water which loses itself in the depths of the ocean, Jesus alone remained; the Master, the King! Had not Thérèse begged Him to take away from her, her liberty? That liberty made her afraid; so weak, so fragile did she feel herself that she longed to be united forever to Divine Strength.

Story of a Soul, *Ch. IV*

I HAD taken as my rule of conduct, to receive most faithfully Holy Communion as often as my confessor permitted, without ever asking that it might be more frequent. I would act differently now; for I am quite sure that a soul ought to make known to her director the attraction that she feels to receive her God. It is not to remain in a golden ciborium that He comes down each day from Heaven, but to find another Heaven, the Heaven of our soul in which He takes His delight.

Story of a Soul, *Ch. V*

WHAT shall I say of my thanksgivings after Holy Communion? There are no moments in which I feel less consolation. And is not this very natural, seeing that my desire is to receive our Lord's visit, not for my own satisfaction, but solely for His pleasure.

I imagine my soul to be as a plot of waste ground and beg the Blessed Virgin to remove from it all the rubbish—meaning its imperfections; then I beseech her to erect thereon, a vast canopy worthy of Heaven and to decorate it with her own treasures, and I invite all the Angels and Saints to come and sing canticles of love. It seems to me then that Jesus is pleased to see Himself so magnificently received; and I, I share His joy. All this does not hinder distractions and sleep from molesting me; therefore it not rarely happens that I resolve to continue my thanksgiving all the day long, since I have made it so badly in the Choir.

Story of a Soul, *Ch. VIII*

AT the time of Holy Communion I sometimes picture my soul under the figure of a little child of three or four years, who at play has got its hair tossed and its clothes soiled.—These misfortunes have befallen me in battling with souls.—But very soon the Blessed Virgin hastens to my aid: quickly she takes off my little dirty pinafore, smooths my hair and adorns it with a pretty ribbon or simply with a little flower . . . and this suffices to render me pleasing and enables me to sit at the Banquet of Angels without blushing.

Counsels and Reminiscences

THE demon, traitor that he is, knows well, that he cannot make a soul who wills to belong wholly to the good God, commit sin; therefore he endeavors only to persuade her that she sins. That is a great deal gained, but it is not yet enough to satisfy his rage . . . he aims at something further, he wants to deprive Jesus of a loved tabernacle. Not being able himself to enter into this sanctuary he wishes that it may at least remain empty and without its Lord. Alas! what will become of this poor heart? . . . When the devil has succeeded in driving away a soul from Holy Communion he has gained his ends, and Jesus weeps. . .

Letter I to her Cousin Marie Guerin

A NOVICE relates that she wanted to deprive herself of Holy Communion because of some lack of fidelity. She wrote her determination to Sister Thérèse of the Child Jesus who thus replied:

"Little flower cherished by Jesus, it is amply sufficient that by the humiliation of your soul your roots *eat of the earth* . . . You must open a little, or rather raise on high your corolla so that the Bread of Angels may come as a divine dew to strengthen you, and to give you all that is wanting to you.

"Good-night, poor little floweret; ask of Jesus that all the prayers offered for my recovery may serve to augment the fire which must consume me."

Counsels and Reminiscences

XVII
Suffering[88]

THE cross has accompanied me from the cradle; but then, Jesus has made me love it passionately.

Letter IX to her Missionary "Brothers"

ONE day my sister Marie, speaking of suffering, said that instead of making me walk by that way, the good God would no doubt carry me always like a little child. These words recurred to me after Holy Communion on the following day, and my heart was

---

[88] No reader should be discouraged by this chapter on Suffering. What St. Thérèse says is very consoling for those who are nailed to the Cross; and others must remember that God had given to His humble Servant a *sensible* attraction for suffering, which is a rare grace and reserved to very few souls, though many imagine they possess it, and mistake their road choosing to follow this supposed attraction. Without the sensible desire and even though experiencing an invincible repugnance to suffer, souls can be sanctified. What pleases God is that the suffering be borne with love.

fired with an ardent desire of suffering. I felt too an inward assurance, that crosses in great number were in reserve for me. Then my soul was inundated with consolations such as I have never had again in all my life. Suffering became my attraction, in it I found charms that entranced me.

Another great desire that I felt, was to love but God alone and to find no joy save only in Him. Often during my thanksgiving after Holy Communion I used to repeat this passage from the *Imitation: "O Jesus, who art ineffable sweetness, turn for me into bitterness all the consolations of earth."*[89] These words came from my lips without effort; I uttered them like a child who repeats without too well understanding, words prompted by a friend.

Story of a Soul, *Ch. IV*

SUFFERING has held out its arms to me from my very entrance into Carmel and lovingly have I embraced it. My intention in coming here, I declared in the solemn examination which preceded my profession: *I am come in order to save souls, and especially to*

---

89 *Imit.*, III, ch. xxvi, 3.

pray for Priests. When we want to attain an end we must employ the means, and Jesus having made me understand that He would give me souls by means of the cross, the more crosses I met with the more my attraction to suffering increased. During five years this way was mine; but I alone knew it. Here was just the hidden flower that I wanted to offer to Jesus, this flower which exhaled its fragrance for Heaven alone.

Story of a Soul, *Ch. VII*

FOR one pain endured with joy, we shall love the good God more forever.

Letter I to Mother Agnes of Jesus

IN my soul's intercourse with Jesus—nothing . . . dryness! sleep! Since my Beloved wills to sleep I shall not hinder Him; I am too happy in seeing that He does not treat me like a stranger, that He is not constrained with me. He pierces His little ball through and through with pin-pricks sore indeed . . . When it is this tender Friend who Himself pierces His ball, the pain is naught but sweetness—so gentle is His Hand. How different when creatures pierce it!

Yet I am happy, yes, truly happy to suffer. If Jesus does not Himself directly pierce His little ball, it is certainly He who guides the hand that wounds!

Letter II to Mother Agnes of Jesus

YES, I desire them, those heart-thrusts, those pinpricks that give so much pain . . . Sacrifice I prefer to all ecstasies: therein lies happiness for me, I find it nowhere else. *The little reed* has no fear of breaking, for it is planted on the shore of the waters of Love; and so, when it bends, that beneficent wave invigorates it, and makes it long for another storm to come and bow down its head anew. My weakness it is, that makes my whole strength. Whatever happens I cannot get broken; I see only the gentle hand of Jesus.

To win the palm no suffering is too great.

Letter III to Mother Agnes of Jesus

THE drop of gall must be mingled in every cup, but I find that trials greatly help to detach us from earth; they make us look higher than this world. Nothing here below can satisfy us; we can enjoy a little repose only by being ready to do God's Will.

Letter I to Mother Agnes of Jesus

MY soul has known many kinds of trials, greatly have I suffered here on earth. In my childhood I suffered with sadness; now, it is with peace and joy that I taste of all the bitter fruits.

Story of a Soul, *Ch. IX*

SUFFERING united to love is the only thing that appears to me desirable in this vale of tears.

Letter IX to her Missionary "Brothers"

WHEN we are expecting only suffering the least joy surprises us: suffering itself becomes the greatest of joys when we seek it as a precious treasure.

Story of a Soul, *Ch. IX*

THERE are people who take everything in the way that gives them the most pain; with me it is the reverse; I see always the good side of things. If I have naught but pure suffering, without any break, well! I make of it my joy.

Counsels and Reminiscences

JOY is not in the things that surround us, it resides in the interior of the soul. One may possess it in the depths of a gloomy prison, as well as in a royal palace. Thus am I happier in Carmel, even in the midst of interior and exterior trials, than in the world, where nothing was wanting to me.

Story of a Soul, *Ch. VI*

IF now, amid trials, and in the thick of the fight, we can already find such delight in the thought that God has drawn us away from the world, what will it be, when in Heaven's eternal glory and never-ending rest, we shall understand the incomparable favor He has shown us in choosing us here, to dwell in His own House—the very threshold of Heaven.

Story of a Soul, *Ch. X*

LET us not expect to find Love without Suffering. Our nature is there, and it is not there for nothing; but what treasures it enables us to acquire! It is our means of gain; so precious is it that Jesus came down upon earth expressly to possess it . . . We want to suffer generously, grandly; we wish never to fall; what illusion! And what does it matter to me if I fall every minute? I find great profit in it, for thereby I see my weakness. My God, You know what I am capable of unless You carry me in Your arms; and if You leave me alone, well; it is that it pleases you to see me *on the ground*, so why should I be disquieted?

Letter V to her Sister Celine

LIFE is often irksome and bitter; it is hard to begin a laborious day, above all when Jesus hides Himself from us. What is this tender Friend doing? Does He not then see our anguish, the load that oppresses us; where is He? Why does He not come to console us?

Ah, fear not . . . He is there, quite near! He is watching us; He, it is, who begs for these our labors and our tears . . . He has need of them for souls, for our soul; He wants to give us so glorious a recompense.

Ah! truly, it costs Him to make us drink of this bitter cup, but He knows that it is the one way by which to prepare us to know Him as He knows Himself and to become ourselves God-like. What a destiny! How great is the soul. Let us rise above all that passes away, let us hold aloof from the earth, up on high the air is so pure; Jesus may hide Himself but one is conscious of His presence.

Letter I to her Sister Celine

WHEN we speak of peace we do not mean joy—not at least sensible joy; to suffer in peace it is enough that we truly will all that God wills.

Letter V to her Sister Celine

NOTWITHSTANDING the trial which deprives me of every feeling of enjoyment I can yet exclaim, *"Thou hast given me delight, O Lord, in all Thou dost."*[90] For is there a greater joy than to suffer for Thy Love? The more intense the suffering and the less apparent to human eyes, the more lovingly dost Thou

---

[90] Ps., xci, 5.

smile upon it, O my God. And even—supposing an impossibility—if Thou wert unaware of it, I would still be happy to suffer, in the hope that by my tears I might perhaps prevent, or make reparation for one single sin against faith.

Story of a Soul, *Ch. IX*

MINE is not an unfeeling heart, and it is just because of its capacity to suffer deeply that I desire to offer to Jesus every kind of suffering it can endure.

Story of a Soul, *Ch. IX*

LIFE is full of sacrifices, it is true; but why look for happiness in it? Is it not simply "a night to be passed in a bad Inn" as says our Holy Mother Saint Teresa?

My heart has an ardent thirst for happiness, but well do I see that no creature is capable of allaying this thirst. On the contrary, the more I might drink of the waters of that enchanted spring the more burning would be my thirst.

I know a fountain where *they that drink shall yet thirst,*[91] but with a thirst most sweet, a thirst one can always satisfy; this fountain is the suffering that is known to Jesus alone! . . .

Letter II to Sr. Marie of the Sacred Heart

OUR Lord never asks of us any sacrifice above our strength. Sometimes, in truth, the Divine Master makes us taste the full bitterness of the chalice which He presents to our soul. When He asks the sacrifice of everything most dear to us in this world, it is impossible unless by a very special grace, not to cry out as He did in the Garden of the Agony: *"My Father, let this chalice pass from Me. . ."* But let us also hasten to add: *"Nevertheless not as I will but as Thou wilt."*[92] It is very consoling to think that Jesus—Divine Strength itself—has experienced all our weakness, that He trembled at the sight of the bitter chalice, the chalice He had longed for so ardently.

Letter I to her Missionary "Brothers"

---

[91] *Cf.* Eccles., xxiv, 29.

[92] Matt., xxvi, 39.

SINCE our Well-Beloved has *"trodden the wine-press alone."*[93]—the wine which He gives us to drink—in our turn let us not refuse to wear garments dyed with blood, let us press out for Jesus a new wine which may slake His thirst, and *looking around Him* He will no longer be able to say that *He is alone*; we shall be there *to help.*[94]

Neglect, forgetfulness . . . this it is, it seems to me, which still pains Him the most.

Letter VIII to her Sister Celine

HERE on earth, where all changes, one sole thing changes not, the King of Heaven's mode of acting as regards His friends. Ever since He uplifted the standard of the Cross, it is in its shadow that all must fight and gain the victory.

Letter II to her Missionary "Brothers"

---

93 Isa., lxiii, 3.

94 Isa., lxiii, 5.

IT is indeed more through suffering and persecution than through eloquent preaching, that God wills to establish His Kingdom in souls.

Letter VI to her Missionary "Brothers"

I WANT to forget this world; here below, all things weary me, I find no joy save one, that of suffering . . . and this joy, though unfelt, is above every other.

Letter V to her Sister Celine

WHEN I suffer much, when things that are painful and disagreeable befall me, instead of assuming an air of sadness, I respond by a smile. At first I was not always successful, but now it is a habit which I am very happy to have acquired.

Story of a Soul, *Ch. XII*

A NOVICE was complaining of being more tired than her Sisters, for besides the common work, she had done another task, of which they knew nothing; Thérèse answered: "I want to see you always like a valiant soldier who does not complain of his pains; who thinks very seriously of the wounds of his brothers and regards his own as mere scratches. Why do you feel this fatigue to such a degree? It is because no one knows about it. . .

"Blessed Margaret Mary having had two whitlows used to say she had only really suffered from the first one, because it had not been possible for her to hide the second from her Sisters, and thus it became the object of their compassion.

"This feeling is natural to us; yet to wish that all should know when we suffer is a very commonplace manner of acting."

Counsels and Reminiscences

DURING the first months of her illness it was on her hard palliasse that Sister Thérèse passed the time of rest, and her nights were very bad: when asked whether she did not need some assistance during those hours of pain, she replied: "Oh, no on the contrary, I think myself very fortunate to be in a cell distant enough for my Sisters not to hear me. I rejoice to suffer alone; but from the moment I am pitied and surrounded with delicate attentions I can no longer feel this joy."

Story of a Soul, *Ch. XII*

THE Sister infirmarian remarking, "It is said that you have never suffered very much." Thérèse smiled and pointing to a glass containing a draught of medicine, bright red in color, replied, "See this little glass, one would imagine it full of some choice liqueur, but in reality I take nothing that is more bitter. Well! it is an image of my life; to the eyes of others it has ever appeared clothed in the most radiant hues; to them it seemed as though I drank a delicious liqueur, while in truth it was bitterness. I say bitterness, and yet my life has not been bitter, for I have known how to make of all bitterness my sweetness and my joy."

"You are in great pain at this moment, are you not?" "Yes . . . but I have so much desired to suffer."

Story of a Soul, *Ch. XII*

HOW it grieves us to see you suffer, and to think you may perhaps have still more to endure," the novices were saying to her.

"Oh! do not be troubled about me, I have arrived at the stage of being no longer able to suffer, because all suffering is sweet to me."

Story of a Soul, *Ch. XII*

A SISTER, who doubted her patience, noticed, when visiting her one day, an expression of heavenly joy on her countenance and wished to know the reason. "It is because of the very acute pain I am feeling," replied Thérèse, "I have always striven to love suffering and to give it a cordial welcome."

Story of a Soul, *Ch. XII*

WHY are you so cheery this morning?" she was asked; "It is because I have had two little trials, nothing gives me *little joys* like *little trials*."

Story of a Soul, *Ch. XII*

ANOTHER time: "You have had a great many trials today."

"Yes, but . . . seeing that I love them! . . . I love everything the good God sends me."

Story of a Soul, *Ch. XII*

AGAIN, when some one said to her: "It is dreadful—all you are suffering."

"No, it is not dreadful; could a little Victim of Love find anything dreadful that her Spouse sends her? He gives me at each moment what I can bear; not more; and the minute He increases my sufferings He also augments my fortitude.

"Yet I could never ask for greater sufferings, for I am too little; they would be my own—my own choosing, then I should have to bear them by myself, and I have never been able to do anything all alone."

Story of a Soul, *Ch. XII*

DURING her long and painful agony she exclaimed: "The chalice is full to the brim. Never could I have believed it possible to suffer so much . . . I can only find the explanation in my extreme longing to save souls . . . Oh! I would not suffer less."

Story of a Soul, *Ch. XII*

XVIII
The Direction of Souls

OUR Lord allowed me the consolation of closely studying the souls of children.

Considering these innocent souls I used to compare them to soft wax, upon which any impression may be stamped the bad, alas! like the good; and I understood those words of Jesus: "*But he that shall scandalize one of these little ones . . . it were better for him that a millstone were hanged about his neck and that he were drowned in the depth of the sea.*"[95] Oh! how many souls might attain to a high degree of holiness if wisely guided from the very first.

I well know that to accomplish His work of sanctification, God has need of no one, but just as He enables a skilful gardener to rear plants that are delicate and rare, granting him for this end all the knowledge necessary, while reserving to Himself the care of giving

[95] Matt., xviii, 6.

the increase, so, too, does He will to be aided in His divine culture of souls.

Story of a Soul, *Ch. V*

AS soon as I penetrated into the sanctuary of souls I judged at the first glance that the task exceeded my powers, and very quickly placing myself in the arms of the good God I imitated the little child, who, seized with sudden fear, tries to hide its golden head on its father's shoulder, and I said: "Lord, Thou knowest it, I am myself too little to be capable of nurturing these Thy children; if Thou dost will to give to them, through me, what is suited to each one, fill Thou my little hand, and without leaving Thine arms, without even turning my head aside, I will distribute Thy treasures to the souls who come to me to seek sustenance. When they find it to their liking I shall know that it is not to me they owe it but to Thee; on the other hand if they complain, and find bitter what I offer them, my peace shall remain undisturbed, I will try to convince them that this nutriment comes from Thee, and I will carefully refrain from seeking any other for them."

When I thus understood that it was impossible for me to do anything by myself, the task appeared to me simplified. Interiorly, I occupied myself solely in trying to become more and more united to God—knowing that the rest would be added unto me.

Story of a Soul, *Ch. X*

FROM afar it seems easy to do good to souls, to make them love God more, to mould them after our own views and opinions. But coming closer one feels, on the contrary, that to do good without the divine assistance, is as impossible a thing as to bring the sun back after it has set. One feels that it is absolutely necessary to forget our own inclinations, our personal notions, and to guide souls, not by our own way—the way we ourselves go—but by the particular way that Jesus wishes to lead them.

Story of a Soul, *Ch. X*

WHEN very young, and staying with my aunt, a book was given to me to read. In one of the stories I saw that the mistress of a school was much praised because she knew how to get on cleverly in the world without offending anyone. This phrase I remarked especially: "She would say to the one, 'You are not wrong,' and to the other, 'You are right;" and while I read I was thinking: "Oh! . . . I would not have acted thus; we must always tell the truth." And so I do, always. Far more difficult it certainly is, for when told of some little vexatious occurrence, it would be easy to lay blame on the absent, and she who complains would at once be pacified. Yes, but . . . I do quite the reverse. If I am not liked, what matter! Let no one come to me who does not want to hear the truth.

Counsels and Reminiscences

THAT a reprimand may be fruitful it must cost in the giving; and it must be given without a shade of passion in the heart.

One must not let kindness degenerate into weakness. When we have blamed justly we ought to leave it so, and not yield to feelings of distress at having given pain. To run after the aggrieved one in order to console her, is to do more harm than good. To leave her to herself is to force her to expect nothing from creatures, to have recourse to the good God, to see her failings and to humble herself. Otherwise she would grow accustomed to being consoled after a deserved rebuke and would behave as does a spoilt child, who stamps and cries, well knowing that this will make its mother return to wipe away the tears.

Counsels and Reminiscences

LET the sword of the Spirit, which is the Word of God, abound in your lips and hearts.[96] If we have to do with a difficult soul, let us not be discouraged, nor ever abandon her. Let us have always "*the sword of the Spirit*" to reprehend her for her faults, and not allow things to pass for the sake of leaving ourselves in repose; let us fight unceasingly, even without hope of gaining the victory. What matter about success! Let us fight on, whatever be the weariness of the struggle. Let us not say: "I can make nothing of this soul, she does not understand; I must give it up." Oh! what cowardice that would be. We must do our duty unto the end. [St. Thérèse in these passages refers to her charge as Mistress of Novices.]

Counsels and Reminiscences

[96] Ephes., vi, 17.

THE novices expressed their surprise at finding that she guessed their most hidden thoughts.

"Here is my secret," she said to them: "I never give you any advice without invoking the Blessed Virgin; I ask her to inspire me to say what will do you the most good, and I myself am often astonished at the things that I teach you. I simply feel in saying them to you, that I am not deceived and that Jesus speaks to you by my mouth."

Story of a Soul, *Ch. XII*

GIVE us some advice as to how we ought to act concerning our spiritual direction," they said to her.

"With great simplicity and without depending too much on assistance, which may fail you at any moment. You would soon be forced to say with the Spouse in the Canticles: '*The keepers . . . took away my veil from me and wounded me*,' it was only '*when I had a little PASSED BY them I found Him whom my soul loveth*.'[97] If with detachment you humbly inquire where is your Beloved, *the keepers* will direct you. Nevertheless, most

[97] Cant., v, 7; iii, 4.

frequently, you will find Jesus only after you have *passed by* all creatures. For my part, I have many a time repeated this verse of the Spiritual Canticle of St. John of the Cross:

Send me no more
A messenger
Who cannot tell me what I seek.
All they who serve
Relate a thousand graces of Thee;
And all wound me more and more,
And they leave me dying,
WHILE THEY BABBLE I KNOW NOT WHAT."

Trans. D. Lewis, M. A.

Counsels and Reminiscences

XIX
The Blessed Virgin

HOW I love the Blessed Virgin! Had I been a Priest, oh! how I should have spoken of her. She is represented as unapproachable, rather ought she to be shown as imitable. She is more Mother than Queen. I have heard it said that all the Saints are eclipsed by her radiant brightness as the sun at rising makes the stars disappear. How strange that seems—a mother eclipsing the glory of her children! I think quite the contrary. I believe that she will immensely increase the splendor of the elect . . . The Virgin Mary! how simple does her life appear to me. . .

Story of a Soul, *Ch. XII*

SOMETIMES I find myself saying to the Holy Virgin: "Do you know, O cherished Mother, that I think myself more fortunate than you? I have you for Mother and you have not, like me, the Blessed Virgin to love . . . You are, it is true, the Mother of Jesus, but you have given Him to me, and He, from the cross gave you to us as our Mother, so we are richer than you. Of old it was your desire that you might be the little handmaiden of the Mother of God; and I, poor little creature, I am, not your servant, but your *child*: you are the Mother of Jesus and you are *my Mother*."

Letter XIII to her Sister Celine

O MARY, if I were Queen of Heaven and thou wert Thérèse, I fain would be Thérèse to see thee Queen of Heaven!

8 September, 1897.

Last words written by Sister Thérèse of the Child Jesus.

XX
Various Subjects

LEONIE, no doubt finding that she was growing too old to play with dolls, came one day to Celine and me, with a basket full of dolls' clothes, odds and ends of pretty materials, trimmings, etc., on which she had laid her doll, saying to us: "There, little sisters—choose!" Celine looked, and took a knot of edging. After reflecting a moment I, in turn, put out my hand saying: "I choose all!" and I carried off basket and doll without further ceremony.

This trait of my childhood is, as it were, a summary of my entire life. Later on when the meaning of perfection began to unfold itself to me, I understood that to become a saint it is necessary to suffer much, ever to seek after that which is most perfect, and to forget self. I understood that in sanctity the degrees are many, that each soul is free to respond to the advances of our Lord, to do little or much for His sake, in a word, to choose between the sacrifices that He asks. Then, as in the days of my childhood, I exclaimed: "My God, I choose all! I do not wish to be a saint by halves; the thought of suffering for Thee does not frighten me, one thing only do I fear—my own will; take Thou my will, for *I choose all* that Thou willest."

Story of a Soul, *Ch. I*

MY Father took me for a pleasant tour during which I began to know a little of the world. Around me all was cheerfulness and delight; I was made welcome, petted, admired, in short, for fifteen days the pathway of my life was strewn with naught but flowers. Holy Wisdom well says that *the bewitching of trifles overturneth the innocent mind.*[98] At the age of ten the heart easily allows itself to be dazzled, and I own that this sort of life had some charms for me. Alas! how well the world contrives to reconcile the delights of earth with the service of God. How seldom does it think of death.

And death, nevertheless, has come to a great many of the people whom I then knew, young, rich and prosperous. I like to go back in thought to their beautiful

[98] *Cf.* Wisdom, iv, 12.

dwellings, to ask myself where are they, and what benefit do they now draw from the castles and parks where I saw them enjoying all the comforts of life . . . And I reflect that *"all is vanity"*[99] *"but to love God and to serve Him alone."*[100]

Story of a Soul, *Ch. IV*

WHAT compassion I have for souls who are going astray. It is so easy to lose one's way in the flowery paths of the world. Undoubtedly for a soul who has risen a little above the things of earth, the sweetness offered is intermingled with bitterness, and the immense void of its desires cannot be filled by the praises of a moment.

Story of a Soul, *Ch. IV*

WE have but life's brief day to save souls and thus to give to Jesus proof of our love. The morrow of this day will be Eternity and then He will render to you a hundredfold for the joys which you

[99] Eccles., i, 2.

[100] *Imit.*, I, i, 3.

have sacrificed for Him. He knows the extent of your sacrifice, He knows that the grief of those dear to you increases your own still more; but to save our souls He has Himself suffered this martyrdom. He too, left His Mother, He saw the Immaculate Virgin stand at the foot of the Cross, her heart transpierced by the sword of sorrow.

Ah! if the Divine Master would but grant to those whom you are going to leave for His sake, a foresight of the glory He reserves for you, the multitude of souls who in heaven will form your train, they would be already recompensed for their great sacrifice in parting with you.

Letter II to her Missionary "Brothers"

THE good God has promised a hundredfold to all who have left father or mother or sister for love of Him. These words are, I know, usually applied to those who have entered the religious state, but in my heart I feel that they were also spoken for the generous parents who make to God the sacrifice of children whom they cherish more than self.

Letter to her Cousin Jeanne Guerin

HOW can a heart given up to human affection be united intimately to God? That, I feel is not possible. I have seen so many souls deluded by this treacherous light, dart into it like the poor moth and burn their wings, then return wounded to Jesus, the Divine Fire which burns without consuming.

Story of a Soul, *Ch. IV*

IN giving oneself to God the heart does not lose its natural tenderness; on the contrary, its love grows deeper by becoming more pure and more Christ-like.

Story of a Soul, *Ch. IX*

THERE are souls for whom God's mercy wearies not of waiting, and to whom He gives His light only by degrees.

Story of a Soul, *Ch. X*

WHEN in the morning we feel no courage, no energy for the practice of virtue, this is a grace, this is the moment to *"lay the axe to the root of the tree,"*[101] depending solely on Jesus. If we fall all is retrieved by an act of love, and Jesus smiles. He helps us without appearing to do so, and the tears which the wicked cause Him to shed are dried by our poor feeble love.

Letter II to her Sister Celine

WE must practice the little virtues. This is difficult sometimes, but the good God never refuses the first grace, which gives courage to conquer self: if the soul corresponds to it she will find that she immediately receives light. I have ever been struck with those words of praise to Judith: *"Thou hast done manfully, and thy heart has been strengthened."*[102] We must first act with courage, then the heart is strengthened and we go from victory to victory.

Counsels and Reminiscences

MY God, how varied are the ways by which Thou dost lead souls. In reading the Lives of the Saints

---

[101] Matt., iii, 10.
[102] Judith, xv, 11.

we find a great number of whom nothing has remained to us after their death: not the smallest souvenir, not a written line. Others there are, on the contrary, like our Holy Mother Saint Teresa, who have enriched the Church with their sublime doctrine, not fearing *to reveal the secrets of the King,*[103] in the hope that souls might know Him better and love Him more. Which of these two ways pleases our Lord best? It seems to me that they are equally pleasing to Him.

All the well-beloved of God have followed the inspiration of the Holy Spirit by whom the Prophet wrote: *"Say to the just that all is well."*[104] Yes, all is well when we seek only the Divine Will.

Story of a Soul, *Ch. IX*

HOW narrow are the thoughts of creatures! When they see that a soul has lights which surpass their own, they conclude that the Divine Master loves them less. Since when, then, has He lost the right to make use of one of His creatures, in order to dispense to His children the sustenance needful for them?

Story of a Soul, *Ch. X*

---

[103] Tobias, xii.

[104] *Cf.* Isaias, iii, 10.

WHEN we are grieved at our powerlessness to do good, our only resource is to offer to God the works of others. In this you see the benefit of the communion of Saints.

Counsels and Reminiscences

THOUGH I do not undervalue beautiful thoughts that seem to unite us to God, I have long understood that we must carefully guard against leaning too much upon them. The most sublime inspirations are nothing without deeds.

Other souls, it is true, may draw therefrom much profit if they testify humble gratitude to God for being permitted to share the feast of one of His privileged children. But if the privileged one were to grow vain of her spiritual riches, if her prayer resembled that of the Pharisee, she herself would become like to a person starving to death before a well-served table while all her guests take from it abundant nourishment, and cast perhaps a look of envy on the possessor of so much wealth.

Story of a Soul, *Ch. X*

THE Well-Beloved has no need of our glorious deeds nor of our fine thoughts. If He desire sublime conceptions has He not His Angels, whose knowledge surpasses infinitely that of the world's greatest geniuses? It is not then either intellect or talent that He looks for here below . . . He has called Himself *the Flower of the Field*[105] to show us how much He cherishes simplicity.

Letter XIV to her Sister Celine

TO keep the word of Jesus, this is the sole condition of our happiness, the proof of our love for Him; and this *word*—it seems to me that it is Himself, since He is called the Uncreated *Word* of the Father.

Letter XVIII to her Sister Celine

JESUS needs neither books nor Doctors of Divinity in order to instruct souls; He, the Doctor of Doctors, He teaches without noise of words.

Story of a Soul, *Ch. VIII*

---

105 Cant., ii, 1.

AT Sext there is a verse which I utter unwillingly each day. It is this: "*Inclinavi cor meum ad faciendas justificationes tuas in æternum, propter retributionem.*" (I have inclined my heart to do Thy justifications forever, because of the reward.)[106] Interiorly, I hasten to say: "O my Jesus, Thou knowest well that it is not for the reward I serve Thee, but solely because I love Thee, and for the sake of saving souls."

Counsels and Reminiscences

IN Heaven only shall we see the absolute truth concerning all things. On earth, even in the Holy Scripture, there is a certain obscurity: it grieves me to see differences in the translations; had I been a Priest I would have learned Hebrew, so that I might be able to read the Word of God in that human language in which He deigned to express it.

Counsels and Reminiscences

---

[106] Ps., cxviii, 112.

WE are not yet in our Fatherland, and temptation must purify us as gold is purified by the action of fire.

Letter XVIII to her Sister Celine

IT is best not to expose oneself to the combat when defeat is certain.

Story of a Soul, *Ch. IX*

GOD is often satisfied with our desire of laboring for His glory.

Story of a Soul, *Ch. IX*

A SOUL in the state of grace has nothing to fear from the demons, who are cowards, capable of flight before the gaze of a child.

Story of a Soul, *Ch. I*

TO the pure all is pure,[107] the simple and upright soul sees not evil in anything, since evil exists in impure hearts only and not in material objects.

Story of a Soul, *Ch. VI*

THE good God has told us that in the Last Day He "*will wipe away all tears from our eyes*,"[108] and without doubt, the more tears to be dried, the greater will be the consolation.

Letter III to Sr. Marie of the Sacred Heart

THE Spouse in the Canticles, not having been able in repose to find her Beloved, arose, she says and went about the city to seek Him, but in vain . . . she could not find Him save beyond the ramparts. It is not the will of Jesus that we should find His adorable Presence without effort. He hides Himself, He envelopes Himself with darkness . . . It was not thus He acted in regard to the multitudes, for we read in the Gospels that the people were in admiration when He spoke.

---

[107] Titus, i, 15.

[108] Apoc., xxi, 4.

Weak souls Jesus charmed by His divine utterances. He was trying to render them strong for the day of temptation and of trial; but small, truly, was the number of His faithful friends when *He was silent*[109] before His judges. Oh, what melody for my heart is that silence of the Divine Master.

Letter XV to her Sister Celine

I HAVE read in the Holy Gospel that the Divine Shepherd leaves in the desert all His faithful flock, to go in haste after the sheep that is lost. How touching is this confidence. He is sure of them, they are captives of love—how could they break away? Even so does the well-beloved Shepherd of our souls rob us of the sense of His presence in order to give to sinners His consolations; or else, if He leads us to Mount Thabor it is for one moment . . . the valleys are nearly always the place of pasture, *it is there He takes His repose at mid-day.*[110] [13]

Letter XVI to her Sister Celine

109 Matt., xxvi, 65.

110 Cant., i, 6.

THE sole crime with which Herod reproached our Lord was *folly* . . . and frankly, that charge was true. Yes, it was folly to come seeking the poor shallow hearts of mortals, therein to make His throne. He, the King of Glory Who sitteth above the Cherubim! Was not His happiness complete in the company of His Father and the Spirit of Love? Why come to earth to seek out sinners and to make of them His friends, His chosen companions?

Letter XX to her Sister Celine

MARY, breaking the fragile vase poured out upon the Head of her Saviour a perfume of great price[111] *and the whole house was filled with the fragrance thereof.*[112]

The Apostles murmured against Magdalene; and this it is which still happens with regard to us: some, even of the most fervent Christians think we (Carmelites) are exaggerated, that like Martha we ought to serve Jesus, instead of consecrating to Him the vases of our lives with the perfumes which are hidden within. And yet what matters it—the breaking of these vases—since

[111] *Cf.* Marc., xiii, 3.

[112] *Cf.* John, xii, 3

our Lord is consoled, and the world in spite of itself is made sensible of the fragrance they exhale. And oh! how necessary are these perfumes to purify the unhealthy atmosphere that it breathes.

Letter XX to her Sister Celine

ONE day when I was in tears," relates a novice, "Sister Thérèse of the Child Jesus told me to acquire a habit of hiding my little troubles, adding that nothing renders community life more difficult than inequality of temperament.

"You are quite right," I answered, "I have thought so myself, and in future I shall never cry but when alone with the good God; to Him only shall I confide my trials, He will always understand and console me."

"Shed tears before the good God!" she replied with vivacity, "take care you do no such thing. Still less, by far, before Him than before creatures ought you to exhibit signs of sadness. He has but our monasteries, this dear Master, to rejoice His Heart; He comes amongst us to find a little repose, to forget the continual lamentations of His friends in the world who for the most part, instead of recognizing the value of the

Cross, meet it with repining and with tears; and would you behave like the generality of people? . . . Frankly that is not disinterested love—disinterested love is *for us to console Jesus, not for Him to console us.*

"He is, I know, so kind of heart that if you weep He will dry your tears; but afterwards He will go away quite sorrowful, not being able to find in you the repose He sought. Jesus loves the joyous heart, He loves the ever smiling soul. When will you learn to *hide* your troubles from Him, or to tell Him in gladsome tones that you are happy to suffer for His sake?"

Counsels and Reminiscences

THE soul is reflected in the countenance: like to a little child always content, your countenance should be invariably calm and serene. When you are alone be still the same, because you are ever in the Angels' sight.

Counsels and Reminiscences

OUR Divine Lord wishes to have His court here below as on High, He desires angel-martyrs, angel-apostles.

Letter XI to her Sister Celine

A SISTER, greatly grieved at seeing her so ill often exclaimed: "Oh, how sad is life!" But St. Thérèse would at once correct her, saying:

"Life is not sad, but on the contrary most joyful. If you said 'How sad is our exile,' I should understand you. It is erroneous to give the name, '*life,*' to that which must end. Only to the things of Heaven, to that which shall never know death, should the true name of '*life*' be given; and in this signification life is not sad but joyful—joyous exceedingly! . . ."

Her own cheerfulness was delightful to witness.

For several days she had been much better and the novices said to her: "We do not yet know of what malady you will die . . ."

"But I shall die of *death!* Did not God tell Adam of what he would die, saying to him: Thou shalt die of death?" (In the French: *"Tu mourras de mort."*)[113]

Counsels and Reminiscences

[113] *Cf.* Gen., ii, 17.

IT is not Death that will come to fetch me, it is the good God. Death is no phantom, no horrible specter, as represented in pictures. In the Catechism it is stated that *death is the separation of soul and body*, that is all! Well, I am not afraid of a separation which will unite me to the good God forever.

Counsels and Reminiscences

ONE day she said to the Mother Prioress:

"Mother, I beseech you, give me permission to die . . . Let me offer my life for . . ." mentioning the intention.

And this permission being refused:

"Very well," she resumed, "I know that at this moment the good God so much desires *a little bunch of grapes* which no one wishes to present to Him, that He will certainly be forced to come and steal it . . . I ask nothing, for that would be to depart from my way of abandonment, I merely beg the Blessed Virgin Mary to recall to her Jesus the title of *Thief* which He gives Himself in the holy Gospel, so that He may not forget to come to *steal* me away."

Story of a Soul, *Ch. XII*

"Will the Divine Thief be coming very soon to steal His little bunch of grapes?" some one asked.

"I see Him afar off, and I take good care not to cry out 'Stop Thief!!!' On the contrary I call Him saying: 'This way! this way!'"

Counsels and Reminiscences

The Chaplain asked me: "Are you resigned to die?" I said: "Ah! Father, I find it would be for living that I should need resignation, but as regards dying, I feel only joy."

Story of a Soul, *Ch. XII*

"You will be placed amid the Seraphim in Heaven," a novice said.

"If that should happen, I shall not imitate them; they cover themselves with their wings at the sight of God. I shall take good care not to cover myself with my wings!"

Counsels and Reminiscences

"UNDER what name should we pray to you when you are in Heaven?" they asked her. She answered humbly: "You will call me 'little Thérèse.' *('petite Thérèse').*"

Counsels and Reminiscences

"YOU will look upon us from the heights of heaven, will you not?"

"No, I shall come down."

Counsels and Reminiscences

"AFTER my death I shall let fall a shower of roses."

Story of a Soul, *Ch. XIII*

Prayers Composed by Saint Thérèse

Taken from The Little Flower Prayer Book—A Carmelite Manual of Prayer,[114] *by Frs. Downey & Dolan, O. Carm., published in 1926 by Carmelite Press, Chicago.* ✠ *Imprimatur: George Cardinal Mundelein, D.D.*

MY ACT OF OBLATION AS VICTIM OF GOD'S MERCIFUL LOVE

This prayer was found after the death of Sister Thérèse of the Child Jesus and the Holy Face in the copy of the Gospels which she carried night and day close to her heart.

[114] *The Little Flower Prayerbook: A Carmelite Manual of Prayer* is available at TANBooks.com.

O MY God! O Most Blessed Trinity! I desire to love Thee and to make Thee loved—to labor for the glory of Holy Church by saving souls here upon earth and by delivering those suffering in Purgatory. I desire to fulfill perfectly Thy Holy Will and to reach the degree of glory Thou hast prepared for me in Thy Kingdom. In a word, I wish to be holy, but, knowing how helpless I am, I beseech Thee, my God, to be Thyself my holiness.

Since Thou hast loved me so much as to give me Thine Only-Begotten Son to be my Saviour and my Spouse, the infinite treasures of His merits are mine. Gladly do I offer them to Thee, and I beg of Thee to behold me only through the Eyes of Jesus, and in His Heart aflame with love. Moreover, I offer Thee all the merits of the Saints both in Heaven and on earth, together with their acts of love, and those of the holy Angels. Lastly, I offer Thee, O Blessed Trinity! the love and the merits of the Blessed Virgin, my dearest Mother—to her I commit this Oblation, praying her to present it to Thee.

During the days of His life on earth, her Divine Son, my sweet Spouse, said unto us: *"If you ask the Father anything in My Name, He will give it to you."* Therefore I am certain Thou wilt fulfill my longing. O my God! I know that the more Thou wishest to bestow, the more Thou dost make us desire. In my heart I feel boundless desires, and I confidently beseech Thee to take possession of my soul. I cannot receive Thee in Holy Communion as often as I would; but, O Lord, art Thou not all-powerful? Abide in me as Thou dost in the Tabernacle—never abandon Thy little Victim.

I long to console Thee for ungrateful sinners, and I implore Thee to take from me all liberty to sin. If through weakness I should chance to fall, may a glance from Thine Eyes straightaway cleanse my soul and consume all my imperfections—as fire transforms all things into itself.

I thank Thee, O my God, for all the graces Thou hast granted me: especially for having purified me in the crucible of suffering. At the Day of Judgment I shall gaze on Thee with joy, as Thou bearest Thy scepter of the Cross. And since Thou hast deigned to give me this precious Cross as my portion, I hope to be like unto Thee in Paradise and to behold the Sacred Wounds of Thy Passion shine on my glorified body.

After earth's exile I trust to possess Thee in our Father's Home; but I do not seek to lay up treasures in Heaven. I wish to labor for Thy Love alone—with the sole aim of pleasing Thee, of consoling Thy Sacred

Heart, and of saving souls who will love Thee throughout eternity.

When the evening of life is come, I shall stand before Thee with empty hands, because I do not ask Thee, my God, to take account of my works. All our works of justice are blemished in Thine Eyes. I wish therefore to be robed with Thine own Justice, and to receive from Thy Love the everlasting gift of Thyself. I desire no other Throne, no other Crown, but Thee, O my Beloved! In Thy sight time is naught—*"one day is a thousand years."* Thou canst in a single instant prepare me to appear before Thee.

IN order that my life may be one Act of perfect Love, *I offer myself as a Victim of Holocaust to Thy Merciful Love*, imploring Thee to consume me unceasingly, and to allow the floods of infinite tenderness gathered up in Thee to overflow into my soul, that so I may become a very martyr of Thy Love, O my God! May this martyrdom, after having prepared me to appear in Thy Presence, free me from this life at the last, and may my soul take its flight—without delay—into the eternal embrace of Thy Merciful Love! O my Beloved! I desire at every beat of my heart to renew this Oblation an infinite number of times, *"till the shadows retire,"* and everlastingly I can tell Thee my love face to face. Amen.

A MORNING PRAYER

O MY God! I offer Thee all my actions of this day for the intentions and for the glory of the Sacred Heart of Jesus. I desire to sanctify every beat of my heart, my every thought, my simplest works, by uniting them to Its infinite merits; and I wish to make reparation for my sins by casting them into the furnace of Its Merciful Love.

O my God! I ask of Thee for myself and for those whom I hold dear, the grace to fulfill perfectly Thy Holy Will, to accept for love of Thee the joys and sorrows of this passing life, so that we may one day be united together in Heaven for all Eternity. Amen.

FOR CHILDREN

O ETERNAL Father, Thine Only-Begotten Son, the dear Child Jesus, belongs to me since Thou hast given Him. I offer Thee the infinite merits of His Divine Childhood, and I beseech Thee in His Name to open the gates of Heaven to a countless host of little children who will forever follow this Divine Lamb.

FOR SINNERS

"Just as the King's image is a talisman through which anything may be purchased in His Kingdom, so through My Adorable Face—that priceless coin of My Humanity—you will obtain all you desire." (Our Lord to Sister Mary of St. Peter.)

ETERNAL Father, since Thou hast given me for my inheritance the Adorable Face of Thy Divine Son, I offer that Face to Thee, and I beg Thee, in exchange for this coin of infinite value, to forget the ingratitude of souls dedicated to Thee, and to pardon all poor sinners.

TO THE HOLY CHILD

O JESUS, dear Holy Child, my only treasure, I abandon myself to Thine every whim. I seek no other joy than that of calling forth Thy sweet smile. Vouchsafe to me the graces and the virtues of Thy Holy Childhood, so that on the day of my birth into Heaven the Angels and Saints may recognize in Thy Spouse Thérèse of the Child Jesus. Amen.

TO THE HOLY FACE

O ADORABLE Face of Jesus, sole beauty which ravishes my heart, vouchsafe to impress on my soul Thy Divine Likeness, so that it may not be possible for Thee to look at Thy Spouse without beholding Thyself. O my Beloved, for love of Thee I am content not to see here on earth the sweetness of Thy Glance, nor to feel the ineffable Kiss of Thy Sacred Lips, but I beg of Thee to inflame me with Thy Love, so that it may consume me quickly and that soon Thérèse of the Holy Face may behold Thy glorious Face in Heaven.

PRAYER

Inspired by the sight of a statue of Saint Joan of Arc.

O LORD God of Hosts, Who hast said in Thy Gospel: *"I am not come to bring peace but a sword,"* arm me for the combat. I burn to do battle for Thy Glory, but I pray Thee to enliven my courage. . . Then with holy David I shall be able to exclaim: *"Thou alone art my shield; it is Thou, O Lord, Who teachest my hands to fight."*

O my Beloved! I know the warfare in which I am to engage; it is not on the open field I shall fight . . . I am a prisoner held captive by Thy Love; of my own free will I have riveted the fetters which bind me to Thee, and cut me off forever from the world. My sword is Love! With it—like Joan of Arc—"I will drive the strangers from the land, and I will have Thee proclaimed King"—over the Kingdom of souls.

Of a truth Thou hast no need of so weak an instrument as I, but Joan, Thy chaste and valiant Spouse, has said: "We must do battle before God gives the victory." O my Jesus! I will do battle, then, for Thy love, until the evening of my life. As Thou didst not will to enjoy rest upon earth, I wish to follow Thine example; and then this promise which came from Thy Sacred Lips will be fulfilled in me: *"If any man minister to Me, let him follow Me, and where I am there also shall My servant be, and . . . him will My Father honor."*

To be with Thee, to be in Thee, that is my one desire; this promise of fulfillment which Thou dost give helps me to bear with my exile as I await the joyous Eternal Day when I shall see Thee face to face.